gay
dating
your guide to finding love

Jaye Sassieni

gay dating

your guide to finding love

the essential read for every gay man

Jaye Sassieni

ISBN 1-4528-1070-2

Printed by CreateSpace. First Edition May 2010

Cover design by den_cb@hotmail.com

www.urbanconnections.co.uk

Contents

Introduction:

For some unknown reason, I have always played matchmaker for my friends, both gay and straight, and been the one they invariably come to for relationship advice (phone calls at 3am asking 'who should pay the bill on the third date?' or 'what does he *really* mean in his text message?') Maybe I have an aura of innate understanding and knowledge about me or maybe I should just turn my phone off! I find that however dating savvy or experienced we become, it all goes out the window when we meet someone who we *really* like and we end up reduced to angst-ridden teenagers, unable to take a step back from the situation and see things clearly. The need for friends to give us advice and a metaphorical slap in the face becomes apparent. This eventually led me to create Urban Connections four years ago, a website which provides events for single gay Londoners. It started as a few of my friends getting together in a coffee shop and has grown to regular events for gay guys who want to make new friends, dates or contacts in a friendly atmosphere. It quickly became clear to me that so many gay guys were having problems trying to find a partner; no matter how attractive, successful or intelligent they are. They all seemed to be facing the same problems and running head on into the same issues. Part of my role when hosting events has always been listening to guys relationship troubles and giving my two pennies worth. I feel privileged that so many guys trust me and value my opinion and these last few years have been the equivalent of taking a degree in Gay Dating, if such a thing existed. I started to run dating coaching sessions with the aim of helping my clients to overcome personal issues, e.g. lack of self-confidence, and examine their beliefs and attitudes towards dating. I am not a therapist, nor a psychologist, but four years of meeting gay men at my singles events, seeing their body language, hearing their stories and gaining a real insight into the problems that affect gay guys today (not to mention several years searching for my own Mr Right) has given me enough material to write a volume of books on the subject. So, after several conversations with my psychologist friend, I decided to put pen to paper (or tap away at my laptop in a gay Carrie Bradshaw kind of way)in a bid to explain what was happening and why so many intelligent, solvent, caring and successful gay guys find themselves single, much to the amazement of their straight friends. Why is it so difficult to meet a partner and settle down in a city with such a huge gay community?

Of course, in a wider context, it seems to be more difficult for straight people to get fixed up too; just look at the explosion of dating websites like Match.com, speed dating, slow dating, date my single best friend, date my mum, date my dog (that's a joke) and so on. People today are more stressed out than previous generations, they are more demanding in regards to who and what they want and they are reluctant to settle for less. Think of your mother or your grandmother and how they met their husbands. For a start, they were surely less demanding compared to people today. Forty years ago nobody would have dreamed of insisting their future partner had a six pack, waxed his back and was a great cook. They met through family, friends or at the local dance. There seems to have been better social cohesion and less single people. Decades of social change (sexual freedom, feminism, single parent families) has altered the way people today view relationships. It truly is a different world.

More recent generations have been brought up with aggressive marketing campaigns urging them to whiten their teeth, loose weight, get a perfect body and buy expensive gadgets to make us feel like we have more control of our lives. We are not allowed to feel content or satisfied because our capitalist, consumer society wants us to keep wanting and buying new things; nothing is good enough.

Bling and money equal success. Teen idols gaze at us from billboards with perfect bodies and images of good looking, slim, happy people are used to sell us everything. So, it's not surprising that people's expectations have risen and, considering the dramatic increase in the number of single households all over the country, they are also prepared to create a comfortable life for themselves while waiting for Mr/ Miss Right to appear.

But, I want to focus on gay men as I believe there are many specific issues that are relevant to us. My intention is not to judge or lay down the law on how anyone should be living, but rather to encourage readers to take a step back and try to look at life and how they approach and do things, how they think about certain things, how they behave or why they feel a certain way. Let me admit from the very start that this book is not supposed to be an easy read. My aim is for the reader to stop and question himself, his beliefs, his habits, his upbringing and what he has absorbed from the world around him. You may not agree with everything in this book or you may well think certain ideas are so simple they are staring us in the face, but it is often the case that we just need reminding or pointing in the right direction. Take what you need from each chapter and keep an open mind. With all the gay bars, clubs, cafes and gyms that exist today it *should* be easier than it is to meet a partner. Today's gay men want answers! Don't fear; gay Carrie is on the case.

My heartfelt gratitude goes to all those who have helped me with this project. All the quotes and stories are real, although the names have been changed to protect the, ahem, innocent. It has been a real journey researching this book. I have had so many frank and touching stories and experiences from my clients and used all that I have learned while running Urban Connections as well as help from my gay friends and my own ten years plus of dating. I have researched ideas from various writers and relationship therapists and come across fascinating theories which have certainly shed light on a lot of things for me. I hope this book will help you to understand yourself, your sexuality and the world around us a bit better as well as helping you to find your Mr Right. Yes, he exists and he is out there!

Chapter 1

Understanding where gay men are coming from.

If you are reading this book you may have come to the conclusion that it is very difficult for a gay man to find a partner and you could well be right. Being gay is fantastic and has many positive aspects but the life path of an average gay man is very different from that of a straight one and a gay boy has to face many hurdles and ordeals which a straight one would not need to. Let us take a brief look at the life of a typical gay man.

Although the gay movement in the Western world has made huge advances over the past couple of decades (e.g. gay men can get married, adopt children and they no longer have to accept discrimination at work), society and religion, in general, still do not like the idea of homosexuality. Without even knowing, many people have internalised this dislike, or even hatred, and unconsciously pass this on to their children. When a young boy develops an interest in his sisters Barbie or dressing in his mothers clothes (YSL and Dior, obviously a gay boy wouldn't touch anything less) or even kisses or shows affection for his little male friends, his parents don't have to say a thing; the look of discomfort or even horror on their face says it all. Even if parents consider themselves liberal and gay-friendly, they want their child to fit in with the macho culture that will dominate his upbringing and they want to look like good parents who have not made any mistakes or done anything wrong to their child. Faced with this unspoken reaction, many gay children assume from a very young age that there is something wrong with them. This insecurity tends to stick with the child through life and manifests itself subconsciously as relationship difficulties when he becomes an adult.

At school many gay children face bullying or discrimination for being different. They are not interested in the traditional sports, like rugby and football, and prefer to surround themselves with female friends. At the onset of puberty, this difference is highlighted even more (all of a sudden rugby becomes more interesting!) Gay children realise that they are attracted to their own sex and that this makes them different from everyone else at school. A common reaction is to hide their real self and try to fit in with their straight peers to distract attention from themselves and avoid bullying. Showing a romantic interest in another straight boy would be cruelly rejected, so this is not an option. He represses his sexuality and emotions, which can hinder his development and, again, cause problems in later life. While his male classmates are learning valuable social and relationship skills that will lead them into adulthood (how to approach their love interest, how to flirt and court girls, how to date and having their first sexual encounters), gay adolescents growth is stunted. While straight boys are talking (and salivating) to each other about girls and how great growing up is, they are reinforcing the social bonds that will support them through life. Gay adolescents either pretend to like girls too or they remain silent and alone. Unfortunately, there is no class for gay kids that will teach them that they are normal, teach them to love themselves and give them an insight into the gay world. There is no way for gay boys to experiment, talk about their first kiss or learn relationship skills. So, the average adolescent gay male can face fear of rejection, low self-esteem, insecurity, feelings of inferiority, stunted development and more stress, all of which will stick with him subconsciously. The homophobia he sees around him becomes internalised. It's hard to stand up and say that society is wrong when you're just 15 years old. This can often lead to gay men making derogatory, bitchy comments about other gay men when they become 'out' as adults; they're just acting out what they've witnessed and absorbed.

As a young adult, gay teens realise that they have to come out to their family and friends at some stage. This daunting, traumatic task would be beyond the imagination of a straight boy of the same age. The shame of guarding a secret and the fear of losing the love and friendship of those close to him is stressful in itself.

Finally, the young adult male makes his first foray onto the gay scene and realises that he has to make new friends. He doesn't know a soul and has to start his new 'gay life' from scratch. Apart from learning a whole new gay vocabulary (words such as top, bottom, cruising etc) he needs to find a way to meet gay guys, except he has no relationship skills and hardly any self confidence. On top of that, he is faced with the temptation of easily available drugs, 24 hour nightlife, pressure to build a perfect body and offers of casual sex everywhere.

Forgive me for dramatizing or exaggerating any of the above (there may be some gay men who have avoided many or all of these problems and enjoyed a perfect childhood) but I just wanted to stress that, considering what he has been through, IT IS NO WONDER THAT THE AVERAGE GAY GUY HAS TROUBLE FINDING A MATE! Don't beat yourself up if you are having difficulty with your relationships. If you have survived all that then pat yourself on the back and treat yourself to another cappuccino with cream on top. Gay men are survivors and have relationship issues which are very specific; maybe you are not even aware of them. The good news is that they can all be worked through.

Before we go any further I would like you to take a quick reality check and make sure that you are in the right place and frame of mind to start dating. If you have just split up with a partner, lost your job, suffered bereavement or if you are depressed, then now is not the time to be looking for a relationship. You need to be ready to focus on someone else and you can't do that if you have other issues in your life to work through. You will not give your potential dates the right impression about yourself and you could even end up feeling worse than you did before if a date is unsuccessful for some reason. On the other hand, if you have a great job and friends, you feel happy and stable in yourself and are ready for some possibly stressful and exciting ups and downs on the relationship rollercoaster then read on.

Chapter 2.

Looking for Love in all the *Right* Places:

How and Where to find him.

As we saw in the first chapter, gay men missed that stage in their formative years of learning how to court, how to behave in a romantic situation and how to date. While straight boys could get an understanding of how courting and dating works from watching any soap opera or film, there were very few, if any, role models or examples of gay men or gay relationships for most gay kids to identify with or to learn from. My one role model was Steven from the soap opera Dynasty, Blake Carrington's gay son. Viewers never really saw much of him and his partner together but the fact that he was 'gay' (whatever that meant, I wasn't even sure as a kid) and on Dynasty was a big thing for me. Meanwhile, the straight kids had Sammy Joe, Alexis, Crystal and Dex; a whole choice of characters and relationships to observe, learn from and identify with. The straight boys learned that the girls wanted to be wooed in a certain way; by flirting, giving a smile and lots of compliments (or for Alexis, running a bubble bath and popping the champagne.) Over time, this feminine influence educated the boys and taught them how to be subtle, flirtatious and gentlemanly if they wanted to get the girl. That contrasts heavily with how gay men meet each other in bars; a hard, cruisy stare leading to almost instant sex. Nobody has ever written a dating manual for gay men so it is not surprising that they use this basic, primordial, lustful stare to attract a mate. One could even argue that a subtle, flirtatious glance would go unnoticed in a gay bar. Think about some of the straight guys you know and imagine the reaction they would get if they tried to get attention from a girl using the 'gay cruising' method. They would get indignant expression and probably a slap in the face!

In fact, the whole courting idea is often skipped as gay men meet and jump straight into bed, then into a relationship with each other. That may have worked fine for you in the past but, if you are reading this book, you probably want to try a different route. Flirting is an art which can be learned and is based on subtly showing interest with eye contact, gently brushing arms, smiling, teasing and flattering your love interest. The idea is to be charming rather than overtly sexual and, unlike cruising, the goal isn't to end up in bed with each other at the end of the night. Of course, cruising has its uses but a subtler approach will give a warmer, friendlier, less sexual impression to the object of your desire.

Try to remember the first time you entered a gay bar or club and the first time you encountered a guy 'cruising' you. That heavy, cold gaze can be intimidating and make the uninitiated head for the nearest exit, as Jamie, a 28 year old colleague of mine, points out:

> *'I remember being terrified the first time I realised a guy was coming on to me in a club. I was 20 and this guy was glaring at me. I tried to look away but he just didn't stop staring. I thought I must have done something to upset him or he wanted to pick a fight with me or something.'*

Jamie is right; straight men will only maintain eye contact with another man when they are about to fight. It's interesting how the courtship of gay men has been simplified and reduced to that same stare. This is probably due to gay men wanting to hide their sexuality throughout history and developing methods to cruise other men which are covert and undetectable to others. Thankfully, nowadays it's OK to smile and say 'hi'; gay men can openly date and get to know each other.

The whole notion of 'gay dating' may seem bizarre or foreign to many gay men today but it is one worth exploring. For others, the whole notion of dating may seem like something straight people do or just plain scary! We are supposed to spend an evening with someone we don't know, make conversation, be funny, make a great impression and then fall in love and waltz off into the sunset. I suggest taking a step back from the intensity of the whole idea of dating and start by just going for a coffee with someone you like. If that goes well then you can go on a 'date' but even then it should be about having fun!

So, let's go back to basics. I am sure you know how gay guys meet in this day and age and the last thing I want to do is seem patronising, but, lets just re-examine where and how it could be possible to meet a guy for a relationship with the intention of maybe correcting any erroneous viewpoints or unproductive patterns. Imagine you are looking at the whole gay world from afresh, leaving your past conclusions and preconceptions aside (like a gay tourist from another planet who has just arrived on his pink tour bus.)

BARS:

Bars and pubs are places to have fun; to meet friends, have a chat and a laugh and, of course, cruise for sex. Although many couples have been formed after meeting in bars, the atmosphere is geared toward fun, loud music, lots of alcohol and hardly anyone has love on their mind. A bar full of men who are anywhere from mildly intoxicated to downright paralytic may not be the best environment to meet potential partners. But, saying that, in the age of the internet it is refreshing to go out and meet new guys face to face. There are no touched up photos or chat windows to hide behind and that's the way it should be. Many guys have found love in noisy bars so there are no hard and fast rules. As the old saying goes; *love comes when you least expect it*! Cupid's arrow could strike while you are queuing at the supermarket or ordering your daily skinny latte so you shouldn't rule anything out, but at the same time be practical and don't waste your time looking in the wrong places.

Imagine how many thousands of gay men there are in this country. Just a relatively small percentage of them consider themselves 'on -scene' (i.e. they regularly go out to gay bars and clubs). So, if you are relying on bars and clubs alone to meet a partner, then you are missing a huge chunk of gay men who could be looking for you but they just don't go out. That's like selling your new brand of ice cream outside a tiny school and ignoring the much bigger one down the road. A 2005 survey (carried out by Out Now Consulting) revealed that 6% of the population or 3.6 million people in the UK are gay and lesbian. That's an awful lot of people and this figure is even higher in the U.S. If you consider half of that figure will be men you are left with 1.8 million guys. Then, if we imagine that one third of all those guys are happily settled, we are still left with 1.2 million gay men. You can be sure that all those thousands of gay guys have different interests and hobbies and, for whatever reason, many of them do not hang around in gay bars and clubs. Daniel, a 32 year old Designer explains:

'I used to go out on the scene but now I mostly just go out with my straight friends. I just got bored of it and it all seemed a bit superficial. Funnily enough, I tend to meet really cool gay guys at music festivals, friends parties and even

through work sometimes. I don't think the gay scene is necessarily a place to meet a guy for something serious.'

As Daniel points out, if you are looking to meet gay guys for a relationship then it's a good idea to cast your net wide and not just rely on gay bars alone. Many guys who attend my events complain of being unable to find a partner in bars. They feel tired of seeing the same old faces and venues every week and complain that everyone they meet tends to be looking for one night stands and nothing more; this is one reason why my events have become so popular. If you spend a lot of time searching for your Mr Right in bars, ask yourself the following questions:

How long have you been going out to bars and how productive has it been?

Are you meeting the kind of men you want to meet?

Do you feel stuck in a rut and tired of the same old faces?

If trying to meet a partner in bars is not really working for you then don't get stuck in the same old pattern. By all means, go out for a few drinks to have fun and see your friends, but consider other methods for trying to find love. If you are standing in a bar feeling bored, jaded and tired, you will not be giving off the right vibes to attract anyone.

Remaining open is important as you never know when you may meet someone who rocks your world. It could be on the bus, in the dentist's waiting room or even walking down the street. Gay guys are everywhere! Demonstrating good body language, smiling and being open and ready to start a conversation is essential. Of all the gay guys I have spoken to while researching this book, the ones who had a relaxed, friendly attitude and could start a conversation with anyone at the drop of a hat seemed to have the most success finding partners.

Body Language

Body language is the key to meeting guys in a bar/ club or any other social situation. Good posture, a friendly expression and a good, positive attitude will go much further than a new pair of designer jeans (we will look at this in more depth later on.)

Whether we like it or not, studies have proved that people judge each other in the first 30 seconds of walking into a room so this is your chance to make a good impression and attract guys to you before even opening your mouth. Very few guys are naturally self confident and can light up a room when they walk in without even thinking about it. Most guys develop techniques of appearing cool and confident; this could be good posture, consciously giving eye contact or walking and moving slowly and with purpose. If Brad Pitt stumbled in to your local bar, hunched over, eyes to the floor and slumped in a dark corner, the chances are that he wouldn't get much attention.

Rob, 38, Engineer.

> *'Low self esteem emits such a negative aura that you don't have a chance until you build your confidence. Some people in bars who aren't confident for whatever reason almost become invisible - you need to be seen and look like you're happy, having fun and enjoying your life and yourself'.*

The other important thing to note about appearing confident is that, even if you feel you can't go up and speak to anyone, you are giving everyone the impression that you *are* open, friendly and inviting conversation. I have seen, many times, a really good looking man with a nice body, dress sense and all the rest in a social situation where he avoids all eye contact. Even if you were to go and stand a few centimetres away from him or give him your sexiest smile, it would go unnoticed because he has shut himself off from the whole room. One of the golden rules when trying to start chatting to someone new *is never start a conversation before you get eye contact with that person*. If he shows a spark of interest then you can go right ahead but, if not, you are risking a rejection (which is not the end of the world and we all need to learn to accept this at some stage) or he could even be straight! If someone wants to talk to you they will give you a sign; a glance, a smile or maybe their body language will be pointing to you.

Try this for yourself; next time you go out, look around at the other guys in the room. Note how they walk into the room, how they stand and interact with each other. Note how confidence is attractive. As Rob remarked, guys who do not look confident tend to appear invisible. Maybe that seemingly invisible guy is the most confident man in the world but he just has bad posture or doesn't care how he comes across. If you feel that you are very self-confident but still have problems meeting guys in social situations maybe you need to think about your body language, your attitude and the impression you are giving. The other side of the spectrum would be over confidence and coming across as arrogant. This would be a big turn off for most guys.

Someone walking with their nose in the air or giving random people a snooty snarl has already cut themselves off from any chance of starting a conversation. Guys who act like this are often over compensating (see the section on low self esteem.) They think that taking on this personage is better than being an invisible, shy guy in the corner.

Approaching guys

When starting a conversation, ask lots of questions (people love to talk about themselves and it takes the onus away from you making all the conversation), give compliments, make that person feel good in your presence. Avoid saying anything negative as you want to come across as friendly and positive. One of my clients told me he tried breaking the ice with a gorgeous guy in a bar by saying *'That barman looks awful in that hat, doesn't he?'* But it turned out the barman and the guy were best friends and he had actually hand-made the hat for him. Keep it positive! Try opening a conversation by complimenting him on his t shirt or tie or asking what time the bar closes. Keep it simple, there is no need for any over orchestrated or corny chat up lines. A simple trick is to give a compliment which also ends with a question. For example:

That's a nice jacket! Do you mind me asking where you got it?

I couldn't help noticing your amazing tattoo; do you get many compliments on it?

Put the ball in his court. His response will let you know if he is interested or not. If he avoids eye contact, gives a one word answer or does not turn to face you then do not continue the conversation. Another way to check if he is interested in you is to invade his personal space bubble. We all have a personal comfort space of around 40cm around us. When people get too close and invade this space, we feel uncomfortable, unless we are attracted to that person. So, after chatting for a few minutes, get slightly closer to him and see if he takes a step back or if he stays put (providing you haven't cornered him against a wall!) Resist any negative dialogues which may be going on in your brain such as telling yourself 'I'm sure he thinks I'm overdressed or fat, etc. Focus on what he is saying and smile. Be a good listener.

Don't put too much emphasis on the conversation; it's just a chat with a stranger at the end of the day. It could result in nothing or it could be the start of a great friendship; keep it in proportion. If he is not interested in you, there are plenty more fish in the sea. The important thing is to get into the habit of giving off a friendly, confident vibe and casually chatting to new guys whenever you go out. The more you do it, the easier and less daunting it becomes and, most importantly, you are increasing your chances of finding a mate.

Of course, it works both ways. It's not just up to you to start a conversation. If someone is interested in you and you have given him eye contact and smiled then he could just as well come up to you and say hello. It doesn't matter who starts the conversation. What often happens is that both parties stay put, waiting for the other one to come over and say *hi* all night! What a wasted opportunity. If you feel you are receiving the right signals then dive in and don't waste time.

Adrian, 29, Student;

> *'In my experience, guys that have a pro-active attitude and make the first move will be the ones that are relationship material. They are showing they are interested and willing to chase you. When I have to do all the work then it never seems to last'.*

Adrian is right; a guy who chases you is clearly interested, confident, sure of himself and may be good boyfriend material but remember that it always takes two to tango!

At some point during the conversation, if you are attracted to the guy you are talking to, you will need to either swap phone numbers or arrange to meet again. Don't put pressure on yourself and keep it light and casual, say something like '*I really want to see that new exhibition next week; it would be great to go together if you are free?*' This type of open question gives him a chance to refuse if he is not interested in you, but also for you or him to suggest another time or another idea if he is busy. A great suggestion is to meet in your lunch break one weekday or just to grab a quick coffee together after work so the meeting is kept brief and you can get to know each other and see each other again without having to spend a whole evening together. If he suggests you add him as a Messenger contact or a Facebook friend, this is a clear sign he does not see you as a partner. If he likes you then he will want your phone number and nothing less.

Never pass up the opportunity to make a new friend. Just because he does not see you as a potential boyfriend does not mean that this won't change in the future. Many great relationships have started as friendships. He will also have many gay friends who could be perfect or know someone who is perfect for you. Just as many people today use networking to forward their careers, think of this as a way to meet your ideal partner. The more contacts you have (and the more that know you are single and looking for a partner), the more chance you have of finding him. But, as I already mentioned, making a positive, friendly impression on these contacts is essential if you want them to mention you to their single friends. Nobody will set up their friends with someone who comes across as arrogant, pushy or unfriendly.

CLUBS:

As with bars, the idea behind night clubs is to go out and have fun! Many guys go out clubbing with a group of friends they will stay with all night and chatting to random guys is not high on their agenda. In many clubs most guys will also be high on drugs. There will be guys cruising, but definitely not for romance. Although you may find the love of your life in a club, the chances are slim so if this is your only way of searching for a partner, you may want to consider other routes.

INTERNET:

Until around ten years ago, bars and clubs were the main way of meeting gay guys. The internet revolutionised gay life and is now the most popular way to meet new guys in your city, neighbourhood or street. You don't even have to leave the comfort of your own home. You can chat with guys on the other side of the globe and search for guys with the same specific interests as you. This has enabled thousands of gay men to find love, sex and friendship at the touch of a button, especially if they live outside the big cities. On the other hand, the problems which internet dating has created include guys who have retreated into a fantasy world. They have online friends, boyfriends and communities; for them the internet has brought an excuse to stay at home and avoid any face to face contact or socialising. This is not healthy or real. It is easier to lie about reality or arrange to meet and stand someone up when you are only chatting with a profile and there is no human connection, guilt or emotion. This impersonal feel in chat rooms and profiles also lends itself to everyday guys posting naked photos of themselves for all to see when in reality they could be shy, retiring people. Another issue (which we will look at again later) is that some guys find it difficult to stop the search as there are so many thousands of guys online and you never know who could be right around the corner. So, the best approach is to use your online profile as a way to meet guys in addition to your normal socialising habits. Be aware that not everyone is being honest and enjoy scanning all the profiles out there but remember what your goal is.

Most sites are more geared up towards meeting up for sex but there are several which are more social. There are online sites that organise real time drinks events for city workers or speed dating events. Other sites allow you to create your own events. Whichever site you choose to use, you will probably need to create a profile. This is a window into your personality and your chance to impress.

Create a successful profile.

Think of your profile as a marketing campaign for yourself. You want to present yourself in the best way possible. Who is your target audience? How can you interest the reader? Is the text short, snappy and enticing? Is the grammar and spelling correct? Have you presented all your qualities, your best characteristics and specified what and who you are looking for? As well as what you want, don't forget to show what you have to offer, for example you could be giving, loving or loyal. Could you use humour to get the message across better? If you are not getting the results you expected, go back to the drawing board and start again, examine what needs to change. Take it seriously as if this was a new marketing project your boss gave you.

Photos

Your pictures are your main selling point; if you can't be bothered to take some decent snaps then don't expect anyone to bother messaging you. Men are very visual creatures and many guys will look at photos in a profile but skip the text. You want to look good but make sure your photos are not misleading; professional snaps are great but photos of you ten years ago when your tummy was flat are a no go, and don't even think of using Photoshop for touching up anything. Keep friends, exes or your mother out of the frame and avoid any posing next to your new car or motorbike (unless you are a sugar daddy searching for gold diggers.) You want people to message you because they are interested in you, not your car or what you own. Think about the impression you want to get across to others; warm and friendly or well-dressed and intelligent? Any topless or naked photos should be avoided; you can still show you have a great body by wearing well cut, flattering clothes.

You may want to ask some friends what they think of the photos you want to use on your profile; it's a good idea to get another opinion. If you don't get the responses you hoped for then try changing them.

Be positive. There is nothing worse than seeing a long list of what a guy doesn't like. Bla bla bla. Who cares? It's a complete turn off for anyone and puts them in a bad light. You want to attract guys to your profile and increase your chances of meeting someone perfect; not turn people away! Emphasise what you do like and what your qualities and interests are. Emphasise that you are not looking for one night stands and you like meeting new people for coffee or a chat. Make your profile pleasant and cheerful to read.

Be honest. Don't lie about your age, your job or anything else for that matter. If your aim is to meet prospective partners then this could prove embarrassing and ruin your chances of success. If you are lying about your waistline or bicep measurements then it could be time to join the gym? Pretending to be something you're not could mean insecurity or lack of self esteem, we will come back to this later. Imagine how you would feel if you had been misled or lied to. Now, let's take a look at a couple of made-up dating profiles.

A bad example of an online dating profile:

GAY DATING PROFILE

No Photo

Height: rather not say
Age: 29
Build: rather not say
Drink: Rather not say
Drugs: rather not say

No photos? Why should
we message him?

No details? What does
he have to hide?

ABOUT ME:
Sane and sorted

This vague phrase is
overused without anyone
knowing what it means!

Work hard, play hard

Great for a deodorant ad
but corny for a profile.

I cant stand camp guys, badly
dressed people, chinese food
or Saturday night TV.

Who cares? This comes
accross as negative
and is a real turn off.

Rugby Build

This means fat.

LOOKING FOR
Sex, Im always horny!

Be clear about what you
want. This is contradictory.

Relationship

Pics to swap

Make it easy for your
Mr Right to find you, this
sounds a bit childish too.

Overall impression: reader has no motivation to message this user.
Move onto next profile.

Now, a much better example:

GAY DATING PROFILE

Height: 5'11
Age: 25
Build: slim
Drink: socially
Drugs: never

ABOUT ME:

hey. chris here.
Im 25 and work in web design in the
West End, and I love my work. I also
do freelance on the side.
Id rather talk to a picture of your face
then your penis....
I cycle. read comics and enjoy life :)

Just seeing what's about on here...
Always cool to go for a drink and meet
people!
Ultimatley looking for a boyfriend.

Selection of clear photos

He has provided all his
stats so we don't need to
ask how tall he is etc.
Mr Right can see straight
away if Chris is his type or
not.

This is friendly, positive,
shows he has a good
sense of humour, interests
and also that he is looking
for more than casual sex.

Overall impression: readers interest is sparked,
they want to know more.

Be clear about what you are looking for.

You can write a great description of yourself, saying how you are looking for the man of your dreams but if you have naked, or even topless, pictures of yourself or if your screen name is 'hornyboy1 ' or 'sexman', then you may have ruined the whole thing. You will attract guys who are only interested in sex. Don't get distracted by other guys looking for sex either, remember why you are on the web site in the first place!

Arranging a date

So, once you have chatted with someone who sparks your interest, the next step is to arrange to meet them. As I mentioned in chapter one, you don't have to consider this a 'date' or put any pressure on yourself. At this stage it could be grabbing a quick coffee together or taking a walk in the park on your lunch break. You just want to find out if there is a spark. If the other guy seems hesitant or keeps making excuses why he can't meet you then don't force anything, its better just to move on. Beware of guys who want to spend hours and hours endlessly chatting on Messenger without any intention of meeting. Many people live lives of fantasy through the internet pretending to be someone else, using fake photos and wasting others time. That is why you should limit emailing and chatting to each other before you meet, just in case he has no intention of meeting you. The last thing you want to do is build castles in the sky, get the wrong impression or end up disappointed due to false expectations. Set the date and wait to do the talking face to face. An important factor to keep in mind is that, before you meet each other, 90% of this man is made up of your own expectations and projections; they are all you have to go on. You don't really know anything about him, especially if you are just communicating through chat screens! You can't sum him up as you don't have any real life clues or signals to go by; another reason not to raise your expectations.

Don't be afraid to ask for a webcam chat; it's the next best thing to seeing him in person and is much better than a photo. You will be able to see him, see how he moves, expresses himself and maybe hear him speak too. If you are not sure about meeting then this could save you time and effort. Try to speak to each other by phone before you meet too; the sound of someone's voice can be a turn on or a turn off. A phone call is also necessary to add a human element to the proceedings! Chat rooms, instant messaging and emails are devoid of any emotion. By speaking to him you will no longer be a two dimensional profile to him and vice versa and he will think twice about standing you up or being dishonest as now you are 'real'. With all the technology surrounding us today, blind dates are a thing of the past! There are a few danger signs to look out for when you do get to speak, here are some classics:

- If he has no photos, is' *having problems uploading'* some or *'they are on his other PC'*, etc; forget it. You are not a blind date contestant. Same thing if he sends you his photos where he is wearing sunglasses and a hat or blurred out of focus.

- If his profile says he is a professional rugby player with a great body but he actually tells you that he hasn't played for a couple of years since a 'knee injury', he is *really* saying he no longer looks like that.

- If he is being cagey about giving you his phone number or insisting you call at a certain time, this could mean he is cheating or maybe married; move on. Especially if he says he wants you to be 'discreet'.

- If he gives any signs of an angry, aggressive personality, a big red flashing light should go off in your brain. Step away and keep moving, there is nothing to see here.

- If he steers the conversation onto anything sexual the first time you speak then he is probably not looking for anything serious.

- If you are chatting to him in a private chat room or on Messenger and he is taking more than a few seconds to respond to you, then he is obviously not interested and has better things (or guys) to do. Forget him. You are looking for someone who is eager to chat to you and responds to your questions straight away rather than someone simultaneously chatting with 20 different guys on his computer screen.

- Look out for any telltale signs that all is not quite right. Does his voice sound much older than the age he told you he has? Do you hear children screaming in the background?

- Beware if he can't give you a date or time for meeting because he is busy with work or has something to do every night for the next five or six weeks. He is obviously not available for any type of friendship or relationship at present. If you are really interested, tell him to call you when he's free. Leave the ball in his court and forget about him for the time being.

- If he asks you how much you earn, what your address is or any details you do not feel comfortable disclosing then politely hang up.

- Use your intuition, if you get even the slightest hint that something doesn't feel right then it probably isn't. Save your time and energy.

Arrange to meet at a bar or cafe or anywhere else that takes your fancy but not at his or your place; that sends a clear signal that it's a sex date. At this stage you want to meet to know more about each other, to see each other in real life and to see if there is any chemistry. The case may be that there are no sparks between you; this could still lead to a great new friendship though. But things may feel awkward if you find yourself sitting on his sofa, glass of wine in hand, desperately thinking of excuses to escape while he is staring at you with hearts in his eyes. Meet somewhere neutral.

Even if you are both consumed with passion upon seeing each other, don't jump into bed straight away. Try to wait for a bit and remember that your goal is a relationship. Sleeping together too early could ruin everything as well as sending the signal that you are just looking for a one night stand.

Other ways to meet gay guys (not for sex.)

As well as the traditional ways of meeting guys like bars, clubs and internet, there are hundreds of groups and clubs where the focus is on shared interests or sport rather than sex; like gay football clubs, badminton clubs, gay men's chorus, gay rugby clubs, gay orchestras, gay swimming groups, dining groups, political discussion groups and cinema groups . Check Google for local groups in your area or just watch the gay pride march in your nearest city; you will be amazed at the number of interesting groups and associations that exist for gay guys. The last Pride march I did in London included the gay firemen's club, gay Jewish association, at least 5 different gay sports teams, the gay Arabic club as well as all the guys that had volunteered to be marshals on the march. These are a great alternative from the gay scene as the emphasis is more focused on friendship but the biggest plus is that everyone is sober!

You don't have to focus exclusively on gay groups either, as I mentioned, there are millions of gay people in the UK and they attend all manner of sports, social, political and charity groups so don't exclude anything. It's always good to make new friends (straight or gay) because each new friend you meet surely has plenty more gay friends and one of them may be your Mr Right. Do not exclude any possibility (social, work or otherwise) for meeting gay guys. If you just have a rigid idea that you can only approach men in bars then you are limiting yourself. Studying something is a perfect way to meet new people and make new friends with your classmates. Sitting next to people on a plane or bus is also a great way to start conversation. If you are religious, you could get involved with your local church (obviously, many religions reject homosexuality so use this to make friends and to meet new people as opposed to hunting men) or a local charity. What about all the time you spend on that stepper machine in the gym every week? You see the same faces every day so why not strike up a conversation?

Are there any gay male areas in your local lido, lake or swimming pool where guys go to sunbathe in the summer or any environment where gay men tend to gather such as the theatre, musicals or art exhibitions? You may find yourself developing new interests along the way and becoming a richer, more cultured person. Practice starting conversations at such events and get into the habit of doing this all the time. Master the art of small talk and making casual conversation with strangers. This can sound daunting to guys who consider themselves very shy, but you can start out with an easy situation; start chatting to the checkout girl while you are shopping in the supermarket or compliment that nice old lady who lives downstairs from you on her new hat. Then, as you become more proficient, you can start to approach guys. Begin by talking with guys you don't necessarily find attractive; just have a friendly chat to pass the time and, ultimately, your goal is to approach the really hot guys that you want to date. Here are a few ideas for approaching guys in everyday situations:

At the bus stop/ train station: *'do you know if the next train goes to xxx?'*

Queuing up in your local café/ store: *'it's so busy in here today, isn't it?'*

In the gym*: 'I've never seen that exercise before; what muscle does that work?'*

Coming out of the cinema: *'great film! What did you think?*

The same thing goes for dress codes. Do not limit yourself by only approaching guys you think *look* gay. Although many gay guys dress in a certain way and you may think you are an expert in spotting them, (combat pants, tight t shirts, etc) there are thousands of gay guys walking around without a label saying they are gay. Of course, I am not saying you should start coming on to random straight guys in the street, but if you get eye contact with a cute guy on the bus or if a gorgeous guy smiles at you in the street (straight guys would never give you eye contact unless they are about to fight you and will almost never smile at you in the street unless they are drunk) then don't miss an opportunity because he is not wearing what you consider to be the 'gay uniform'.

A more direct way to meet men who are guaranteed to be looking for a relationship, rather than a casual one nighter, is speed dating. Although many gay guys initial reaction to these events is ridicule or derision, it really does make perfect sense. Why sit through a bad date with someone for at least three hours and waste the whole evening when in the same amount of time you could meet around 30 different guys! This method of dating is particularly popular with busy professional guys who do not have a lot of time to spend on hit or miss dates. There is no hiding behind touched up photos on the internet and there is the huge advantage of hearing each other speak, seeing each others characteristics and behaviour. If speed dating is too intense for you, you could try wine tasting or many other dating events out there. You have nothing to lose and everything to gain! These types of organised events are also perfect for shy men who need a gentle 'push' to get out there and meet new people. They are also great confidence boosters.

The internet has taken over from personal ads in newspapers or magazines but they still exist. One of the advantages of an ad is that you know that person is serious about meeting a partner because he has paid quite a lot of money (especially if it's in a national newspaper, where you pay per word.) The disadvantages are that there are no photos so you have to rely on his description of 'tall, dark and handsome'. It's easy to see why the internet is an easier option.

The final way I want to mention is using your existing friends help. Your friends and family know you well and they may be the best people to set you up on a date.

Daniel, 36, Account Manager.

> 'I met *my last two partners through friends of friends.*
> *Where there's a connection, friend or work colleague,*
> *I think there's a higher chance of meeting Mr Right*
> *for a lifetime partner. After all, friends/ people close*
> *to you know you best and would only try to begin*
> *introductions if they thought it felt right*
> *and potentially work out. For me, it's a much better*
> *way to meet guys than going on the gay scene'*

All it takes is a word in the ear of your best friend to get the ball rolling. He or she will think of all the people who could be suitable and spread the word. Let your friends and family know you are looking for new dates, maybe they don't even know that's the case. Maintaining good friendships is essential, not just for their help in setting you up, but also for their support and advice on your dating journey (and hopefully you can do the same for them.)

Chapter 3.

Playing and Winning the Dating Game

Let's now imagine that you have found a nice, interesting guy and you have arranged a date in a neutral place. You are both interested in finding out more about each other and there is physical attraction, so half the battle is already won, but it is still very easy to blow it. If you are serious about this man and making a good impression, then there are some small things to recap on which could make or break the date. If you are reading this book because you are having dating problems then now is the time to treat the whole dating process seriously rather than leaving things to chance and hoping for the best. You wouldn't leave an important job interview to chance so why do it with the opportunity for a potentially life changing relationship?

Preparation.

- It goes without saying that you want to impress your date so make sure you plan what you are going to wear. Be sure you leave yourself enough time to get ready and look well groomed. Put some thought into your outfit the day before. Make sure you will not be over/ under dressed. Maybe even ask an honest friend's opinion. If you are looking for a smartly dressed partner who wears suits and shirts then don't turn up in a track suit. Likewise, if you are looking for a rugged, macho hunk then turning up with your handbag over your shoulder may not be the best way to snare him. Opposites can attract, but, in my experience, that is the exception.

- Pick clothes that emphasise your good points but try not to go over the top. Just as a girl wouldn't wear a mini-skirt if she wanted to avoid coming across as too sexual, don't reveal too much (even if you do have a sexy bulging chest.) It's better to hold back. Do you want him to be interested in you because of *you* or because of your biceps?

- No garlic or anything else that could make you smell bad beforehand or during the date.

- Avoid the temptation to have a drink (or even worse, drugs) before you meet for 'Dutch courage'. You may feel more confident when you are half drunk but that's how you will also look to everyone else; half drunk. If you feel you really need to drink before meeting someone, then you need to work on your self esteem.

- Check the mirror before leaving the house for any dandruff on your shoulders, shaving cuts or anything stuck to your teeth.

- Arriving late is rude and will give the impression you don't care so allow plenty of time for your journey. **If you are running late, then an apologetic text message or call is essential.**

Etiquette.

Now, let's look at etiquette (wonderfully old-fashioned but none the less important.) If you have been invited to dinner then a normal reaction for many guys would be that they split the bill 50/ 50. If that's the case then both parties should have a say in the choice of restaurant as maybe one can't afford a huge bill at the end of the night while this is no problem for the other. If one party will be paying for the whole meal then that also needs to be made clear at the invitation to avoid situations like the following:

John, Event Organiser, 28.

> *'I had a date in one of the most expensive restaurants in town with this guy who invited me for dinner. Just walking into the front door I could see it was very chic and as he didn't even give me any say in the choice of venue before he booked, I assumed he was treating me. I tried to choose the least expensive things on the menu as I didn't want to abuse his hospitality but he kept insisting I order pink champagne, etc. When the bill came his face turned green. He didn't have enough money and I had to pay half. He even called the manager over to minus the service charge and he actually asked the manager to bring over a calculator! It was so embarrassing. I never saw him again.'*

John's date was probably trying to impress him by choosing a fancy restaurant which was way out of his league but this can easily backfire, especially if you don't keep track of the prices on the menu! In this case, John had no say in the choice of restaurant so he cannot be held fully responsible, but before entering the restaurant it needs to be clear who is paying. Unlike the straight, somewhat outdated idea of the man always paying for the woman on a date, it is trickier with two gay men and as I have mentioned several times already, communication is everything! Don't be afraid to clarify; it's better to be clear on these small but important details rather than ending up with awkward situations!

The big date.

- The idea of a date is to get to know each other, so relax and be yourself.

- Don't try to tell witty stories and jokes if this is not what you usually do. He is on a date with you because he is already interested, so there is no need to pretend to be anything that you are not.

- Keep the conversation away from anything which could cause any friction or arguments such as politics, religious views etc. Be positive and don't slag anyone off or deride anyone. This is not the time to moan about your boss, your job or your next door neighbour.

- Relax, but also keep in mind that he is using whatever you say to build up a picture of you in his head. Your dirty jokes and strange hobbies can wait till he knows you better; you don't want to say anything which may scare him off.

- Give your date genuine compliments (but don't be cheesy!)If he has nice hair or a great smile then tell him.

- Remember body language; we will look into this in more depth later on. Little things such as giving him regular eye contact (without constantly staring at him as this is off putting) and making sure you don't fold your arms or legs (as this creates a barrier) can make a huge difference.

- Remember to smile.

- Don't talk about your ex; the last thing you want to do is give him the impression you have emotional baggage.

- It is normal and natural that there will be some moments of silence during the date. Don't panic or say the first thing that comes into your head to avoid this. Some guys make the mistake of talking too much when they get nervous. If this sounds like you then make sure you give your date the chance to speak!

Marcus, 26, Student.

'I was going out with a really nice guy who was a teacher. He was so intelligent and interesting and his mind worked so fast that he would already be on the next subject before I even had a chance to respond to his last point. It was always a one sided conversation and it got very boring and frustrating.'

Although I mentioned earlier that you should be taking the organisation of your dates seriously, a bit like a job interview, the actual date should be fun! This is not a casting and there is no need to feel nervous; the worst that can happen is that he may not want to see you again. OK, so you could slip on a banana skin and rip your trousers off but it's unlikely; don't waste time on worse case scenarios. But some guys are naturally very shy and cannot keep their nerves at bay. If this is the case remember to keep your hands away from your face and don't fidget. If you are standing then keep your feet apart and don't shift your weight back and forth as this all conveys nerves. You may even mention to your date that you feel a bit nervous. This could break the ice and it makes you come across as honest and personable. Shyness can be an endearing quality to posses.

One final point which often goes un-noted: TURN OFF YOUR MOBILE PHONE and don't put it on the table/ bar/ cinema arm-rest. Taking calls while you are on a date sends a message that you have other things on your mind and can look arrogant and rude. Even if you are running a huge global corporation, you are dedicating a couple of hours of your busy life to this person so at least pay them the respect and full attention that they deserve! Leaving your cell phone on the table also comes across like you are waiting for something and not fully 'there' in the moment and looks as if you have more important things to do. Whatever the culture is at your place of work this is a huge no no.

If you feel that the date went well, make sure you hint at wanting to see him again. A kiss would be the ideal way to end the night but don't force anything. A touch of the hand or a tender embrace is also fine but if the date finishes with nothing at all, maybe he is not interested? Read his body language. Is his body facing you when he is speaking to you or is he facing in another direction, looking away? When he responds to your question about wanting to meet again, does he say *'yea, sure'* while touching his nose or rubbing underneath his eye (signs of not telling the truth.) While it is polite to send an after-dinner text message thanking your date for the evening, this is not to be taken as an indicator that he wants to see you again. That is why examining his body language is so important; it never lies. There are many great books available where you can learn more about this fascinating subject and simplify your love life no end!

You could also send a text message saying how much you really like him and want to have another date. This is the perfect chance to get some feedback too. A couple of after-date texts are fine, but don't go overboard and bombard him with messages as you don't want to come across as a stalker or too desperate. At this stage you can't really judge if he would be the type to love long soppy text messages with kisses or short, discreet ones. So play it safe and keep it short.

If you were the one that asked him out and arranged everything this time then leave the next date to him. The ball is now in his court to show his interest. Any type of friendship or relationship works both ways; it cannot be one person running after the other one all the time. If he agrees to see you again but whenever you try to fix a date he says his sister is in town/ he is too busy at work/he has a headache, just take a step back and leave it to him while you focus on something else.

If the date did finish with a passionate kiss, do not be tempted to go back to his or your place! Remember you want to get to know him as a person before deciding whether to start anything with him. Sex confuses everything and can ruin the whole relationship before it even begins. Don't rush it; you both have plenty of time (unless he is moving to Peru the next day, which would be the only exception.)

After several successful dates together, if you invite him back to your place then bear in mind that your home says a lot about you. Not just how clean or dirty it is but the decor, the rows and rows of cosmetics on the bathroom shelf and the book collection. Are there any unusual ornaments or strange book titles which could scare him off?

Jason, Supervisor, 43.

> *'When Chad invited me back to his place for the first time he showed me his collection of 'Toy Story' toys. There were hundreds of little green aliens everywhere. When I went to the bathroom it was crammed with every kind of fake tan, make up, face crème and eye gel you could imagine. He must be so vain. I was so turned off.'*

Try to see your home from a stranger's point of view. What does it say about you and what will it be saying to your guests? This could be a make or break factor in your relationship. On the other hand, if you are invited back to his place then it's a perfect opportunity to get an insight into him! Unless he hid the axes under the bed and binned the 7 month old carton of milk in the fridge before you arrived. None of us want to judge our date after seeing a jar of fake tan but, at this stage, we have nothing else to go on and we can easily jump to conclusions. It could belong to his flatmate!

Rejection.

If you don't receive any text messages or calls from him post-date this probably means he is not interested. Try sending **one** text message a week later just to say hi. If you really liked him then it is normal at this stage to make up all kinds of excuses for him like;

- *he is probably too busy at work to text me*

- *he may have lost my number*

- *his life is so hectic*

- *he could have broken all his fingers in an accident and can't text me*

Take a reality check and make life easy for yourself; a text message takes a few seconds to send and I'm sure even President Obama texts or calls his wife and friends several times a day as well as running the country. If his fingers were broken he could ask a friend to call you and hold the phone to his ear in hospital. When somebody really likes you and wants to see you again it feels natural and there is no delay or need to think of excuses. It could be true that he is super busy, lazy or maybe he hasn't thought about you for a week but do you want to start something with someone like that? Do not be tempted to keep sending him text messages or calling him weeks after the date. This will come across as needy and desperate. You need to accept he is not interested and move on. There are plenty more fish to fry and you deserve to be with someone who wants to be with you and appreciates all your fabulous qualities! You can't make someone like you and it doesn't mean that there is anything wrong with you if they don't. Imagine if you did persuade him to start a relationship with you by bombarding him with texts and stalking him; it could only end in tears, probably yours!

Try to learn from the date. Could you have done anything better? It would be ideal to get some feedback from your date, however, most normal, well educated men will make up a polite excuse rather than wanting to hurt your feelings by saying 'I thought you were too loud/ fat/ boring'. Try to discuss the date with a good, honest friend or even a dating coach. Can they spot any mistakes you could have made or anything which could have turned him off? You can't please everyone all of the time and it's normal that for every ten dates you have, maybe you don't click with 40 or 50% or those guys. However, if you find yourself with a zero success rate for those ten dates, then you really need go back over each date with a fine tooth comb to try to see what went wrong. Don't beat yourself up about it or become paranoid and try to see the whole experience as a learning curve. You have no way of knowing what he is *really* searching for deep down so there is no way of covering all options to try to please him.   Now is the time to get back out there and meet more new guys to date and, above all, do not let this affect your self confidence for one second. You are a fabulous, unique individual who deserves the very best. Your Mr Right is out there. Go get him.

On the other hand, maybe *you* did not really feel he was the one for you. In that case then treat him as you would like to be treated; send a polite text thanking him for dinner and maybe say that you would like to remain friends or something of that nature. Do not keep him guessing or waiting for your call and don't just ignore him and hope he will disappear. Remember karma; everything comes back to you so treat him with respect. If you are unsure of how you feel then don't make any snap judgements. You could arrange to meet him for coffee a second time so you have a chance to think about him and make a decision as to whether you want to start anything with him or not. It is not always a case of love at first sight.

Maybe there is a niggling problem such as the fact he smokes or bites his nails. This is understandable but do not let this overshadow all the positive aspects about him. Take your time to think about it. Don't put any pressure on yourself; just make sure that your date does not get the wrong impression. If you definitely decide he is not for you, but you don't know how to let him down gently; try one of the following:

- *'I want to be honest because I really think you are such a great person, I just don't see us together. I want us to stay friends though, if you want to?'* Don't offer to be friends unless you mean it though.

- *'I'm just not over my ex yet, I can't date anyone else'.* This is a white lie but it's better than ignoring his calls and saying nothing.

- *'This is not working for me; I don't think we click together. I wish you the best of luck.'*

Much of this last chapter will seem like common sense to many of you while others will be amazed by new ideas and revelations that they had never thought about before. At the end of the day, dating someone you like should feel natural and fantastic and, somehow, we can just feel when it clicks and falls into place.

Chapter 4:

What type of Dater are you?

Which of the following statements reflect your current thoughts toward dating? Pick one, or more, of these hearts and come back at the end of chapter 5 to see if you have a better understanding of your dating behaviour.

1) I always attract the wrong kind of guy and it never works out for me! Most gay guys are only looking for sex anyway.

2) I've been single for ages and I'm fine with it. I'm not desperate and I'm not going to settle for second best, after all, I'm a great catch!

3) I have a really fixed, definite type of guy that I go for (ie. handsome, nice body.) If a guy shows interest in me, who does not correspond to my perfect type, I'm just not interested.

5) I worry about never being able to meet anyone. I feel anxious and a bit desperate.

4) I'm looking for a boyfriend, but I get distracted; there are so many cute guys and so little time!

6) Sometimes I don't believe
I can have a relationship,
Who would want to date me?

7) I don't want my partner to be too
available.I regularly respond to text
messages a day or so late
so he will think I'm busy; you have to
play the game!

8) When I see my straight friends and family getting hitched,
I feel a pressure to settle down.
I am at that age where I should be going steady.

9) I always go for the wrong type
again and again and again
I just dont know why.

10) Every time I go out with a guy
I can never get past the first
couple of months.

Chapter 5.

Common Barriers to Meeting a Partner.

It seems like there is more gay visibility today than ever before. Your hairdresser is gay (err, obviously), your dentist is gay, many TV presenters, actors and politicians are gay. You can choose a gay law firm or even a gay estate agent. Check out the thousands and thousands of gay guys who attend pride festivals in major cities and it would seem easy to meet a partner. Surely there are plenty of guys to go around for everyone? But this is not the case. There are some barriers to meeting a partner which are obvious; if you lived on a remote island then the problem would be geographic. If you jet off to Peru to search for your future husband without speaking Spanish then that's a linguistic barrier but there are some more frequently occurring, subtle barriers (which are often sub-conscious) that prevent many gay guys from finding their dream man. Let's take a look at the ten major pitfalls which face gay men today. You may recognise some of these pesky obstacles in yourself, your friends or those around you.

BARRIER No. 1: No Rules to Break.

No rules? That's a good thing, isn't it? Straight people from every country and culture on the planet have guidelines, traditions and practises to follow when it comes to courting. Everyone knows the score, what they need to do and what the goal is. However, gay people are only just gaining recognition today and society doesn't yet know what to make of us. With no stereotypical straight role to follow, i.e. get married, start a family, move in together, save up for kids education etc , gay men can make up the rules as they go along (much to the envy of many straight men!) There is no pressure or age limit for finding a partner and staying single has no stigma, in fact, you could say it's the norm. Gay guys can go clubbing and get high every night of the week until they are pensioners, squander all their wages in the most expensive boutiques wearing a feather boa and have multiple sexual partners without being judged by society.

Imagine society's reaction to a 40 year old single mother doing the same thing. Shock horror! On one hand that's great; gay men are the outlaws! How exciting. On the other hand, dating is really just a game; imagine playing Monopoly or Twister with no rules? The whole thing would end in disaster and, despite more openness and tolerance towards homosexuality today and new technologies (like internet dating which should make things easier), that is how many gay men's love lives *are* ending up.

There is no model for a gay relationship. Gay guys do not have to share the same household, they don't have to get married, and they can even chose to have an open relationship. Unlike straight relationships, where the goal would be marriage, children etc, the goal of a gay relationship can sometimes be unclear. So the definition of a gay relationship really comes down to the individual. While gay guys are very sure what their sexual preferences are or what kind of work they enjoy, many gay guys come unstuck when they start dating because they have not thought about what type of relationship they want beforehand. It is important to be clear on this before you start seeing anyone in a romantic way. Do you want a monogamous relationship? Does your partner have to be the same religion as you or share the same political views?

Do you definitely want to have children and expect your partner to bring them up with you? Does your partner's income matter to you? Do you expect him to drop everything and go travelling with you? It is very common for two gay guys to meet, get carried away with physical attraction and great sexual chemistry, start a relationship and then later realise that they have very little in common or they want different things from a relationship.

In a straight relationship there are very clear roles assigned to the man and woman. The man, traditionally, will be the breadwinner while the woman will bring up the children. In a gay male relationship this is irrelevant. Both partners need to work out the best way for them. Our culture does not provide us with any stereotypes to follow for a gay relationship. Which partner should do what? After the first few dates and flush of passion, it is normal that both parties start to work on how they fit together and what does and does not work. While this may be challenging at first, it ultimately leads to compromise and freedom from the fixed heterosexual model. Both guys can take turns being the dominant male- that's fine. One could even argue that this freedom leads to a healthier relationship than the heterosexual norm.

Distractions coming from the gay scene.

Monogamy is often incompatible with many gay guys' lifestyles and that's great for some but not so great for others. Why stay with one partner when there is so much choice out there? There's the internet, diverse gay scenes in most major cities, gay gyms, gay saunas, gay chat lines and gay holiday resorts. This is a dream for many guys; their attitude is that there's too much fun to be had, they can settle down later. The problem is that later often turns to *never* as they get trapped in a cycle of going out, cruising and casual sex. Many gay men start out with the intention of meeting a partner when they are young but they get distracted by all the choice and fun available on the gay scene. Why spend a whole evening dating one guy when you could spend that time scanning through 200 online profiles, making dates and rejecting other potential partners at the touch of a button without even having to say a word? Why stay in and watch a DVD with someone when you could be missing the sexiest guy ever down the local sauna? The adrenaline rush of fast, no strings sex can become addictive. It can come along at any time and there's no time to waste! If you start clock watching when you are away from your online chat screen, if a 'date' means sex or if you often find yourself making excuses to get away from friends or family to go cruising, then this is a definite barrier to you meeting a partner. It could be that you are not the settling down type and that's fine, but if you are reading this book then that is probably not the case. Everyone has seen that 60 year old gay guy, high on drugs in the middle of the dance floor every night and that's great! He's having a ball and we live in a free country where people can do as they please. But do you want to be that person in X number of years? If you feel you have come off the rails at some point then the first step to getting back on the right track is to acknowledge it! We all have the power to choose how we live. Changing your lifestyle and attitudes takes time and there's no time like the present. You are in the driving seat! Tarik, 29, expresses what many gay men feel:

> *'At the moment I don't want commitment, I love cruising and being free but I know the day will come when I don't get attention anymore and then I know it will be difficult to change and try to find someone to settle down with. Not sure how I'll deal with that or even if it will be possible 'cause I'll always have that need for excitement at the back of my mind.'*

As we saw earlier, gay boys often miss out on the normal development and experiences that straight boys go through, for example male bonding through sports or drinking. When they emerge onto the gay scene they often feel they have finally found a way to bond with a group of men who are just like them in massive nightclubs, in many cases where drugs heighten the experience. They feel accepted and that they have found somewhere they fit in. This can be a very positive thing, but some gay men become trapped in the 'eternal adolescent' syndrome. They want to re-live the boyhood that they missed out on and they do all the things that teenagers do such as experimenting with sex, drugs and alcohol, going out every night, buying the latest gadgets, trendy clothes and generally being self-centred. This type of guy tends to avoid any relationships which are long-term or stable because they seem to him as too 'grown up' or boring and mean that he will have to act in a mature, adult way if they are to succeed. If this sounds like one of your barriers that is preventing you from finding love, you may want to examine your behaviour and emotions, possibly with the help of a therapist. The scared, inner adolescent needs to be reassured and gently led by the hand into adulthood. Being in a relationship doesn't mean the party's over, but it does mean being an adult.

Confusing sex with dating.

Straight dating would typically involve a couple going out on several dates before sleeping together. During this time, both parties get to know each other and decide if there is enough common ground and interest for starting anything. Before creating the emotional links that come with sex, the female definitely wants to be sure that the male is stable, looking for more than a one night stand, that he has no emotional baggage and that he is not a psychopath, or even worse, a Barbra Streisand fan! Once a couple have started sleeping together then things become more emotionally complex and feelings get in the way of making rational decisions. As we have discussed, down the road in Gayville, this dating path is not followed. Often, gay guys meet and sleep together straight away. While a straight woman wants to avoid being seen as 'easy', there are no rules to follow for gay men and nobody gets judged as 'easy' for sleeping together on a first meeting. After all, sex is much easier to find when you are gay and it's no big deal. We have instant coffee, fast food, instant information from the internet so why shouldn't sex be instant too? Sex is certainly ingrained deeply into gay culture and for many gay men there is always an expectation of sex at the end of a date. To them it seems strange, unnatural or 'un-gay' to hold back.

Joe, Admin Assistant, 34.

> *'Nobody goes out on dates anymore! I wouldn't even know how to get a date. I never get past that first couple of rushed meetings in a bar with a guy I like'.*

When two gay men initially meet for a drink/ coffee/ dinner date, find that there is mutual physical attraction and rush off home to bed as they can't resist each other, they are skipping the important part of getting to know each other and understanding what each other are looking for. The next day, they wake up together in each others arms and, *bam*, consider each other boyfriends; but they aren't yet. That is a classic mistake; they don't even know each other. They confuse a great sexual connection with a relationship. This is another symptom of many gay men's lack of courting and relationship knowledge. Sex should not be the entry point to a relationship as the following story illustrates:

Billy and Buddy met for a beer after chatting online and immediately hit it off. They ended up in bed with each other that same night. After a couple of weeks of great sex and staring into each others eyes, Billy tells Buddy, in casual conversation, that he has two kids. A few days later, Billy finds out that Buddy has spent five years in jail. Then Buddy finds out that Billy was always looking for an open relationship, monogamy is not his style. The whole thing starts to go downhill as secrets and surprises come out of the closet. A month later it's all over and both are back on the internet looking for new dates.

A period of getting to know each other and understanding what your date wants from any eventual relationship could have avoided these 'shock revelations', hurt and wasted time and energy. Before using the word 'boyfriend', make sure that you are both looking for the same thing and everything is clear. Does Billy think they are dating each other exclusively while Buddy assumes its ok to date other guys? Was this discussed or did one party just assume this?

It does seem a bit scary to talk about relationships when you are with someone new (I don't mean on the first or second date, but after a month or so) and it's understandable that you don't want to kill the spontaneity or passion but that one little conversation is critical. Try to take a 'buffer' time zone of a month after you meet each other, where you just get to know each other; go out and have fun without any 'boyfriend' or 'partner' labels. The following two quotations stress the importance of communication at the start of any relationship:

David, Account Manager, 42.

> *'I spent many years going through a cycle of month long relationships. I would meet some gorgeous guy, we would start going out together but it would always fizzle out so quickly. With experience, I now see that we jumped into things too fast; it was all about passion and the moment and not about dating! I'm not even sure gay men do dating? Pillow talk doesn't count!'*

Jason, Sales Supervisor, 26.

> *'It's easy to get hurt and you can read the signs so incorrectly when you're faced with someone you fancy the pants off, and suddenly you grow blinkers, but don't even know it. You get sucked into bed together, have the best time, you think he's the one, you've found your man, he's amazing, then you don't see or hear from him again'.*

Spending an evening getting to know somebody new does not have to end in bed. Despite the lack of rules for gay men and the huge importance that gay culture places on sex; it does not have to appear on the menu!

Lack of effort.

If a gay man has a disastrous date he can go home and log into any one of many websites to find a second date for the same night in a matter of minutes. He may even see that the same guy he just spent the evening with has also logged back in and is on the lookout again. A friend of mine recently explained how he always takes his laptop with him when he comes into town for a date and keeps it in the boot of his car; that way, if the date goes wrong, he can go back to his car, log back in and find someone else in the same area. Smart, eh? The absence of society's rules and judgements lends a refreshing freedom to a gay mans dating possibilities. **The big downside is that this detracts from the value of meeting someone new**. Gay men know that there can always be someone new just around the corner if they are not 100% happy with the person they are seeing. So this can lead to not putting in enough effort to get to know the person they are currently dating. It is too easy to give up rather than try to understand different viewpoints and stick with a particular guy to see if anything can develop. What often happens if that once a guy finds out his current boyfriend likes a different kind of music to him or doesn't get on with his friends, then he dumps him without a second thought.

Reda, Merchandiser, 32.

> *'One of the great loves of my life dumped me after 4
> months together because I didn't watch 'Coronation
> Street' (his favourite soap opera.) The underlying
> reason was that English is not my first language so I
> didn't really understand a lot of soaps but for him, I
> think, he just didn't want to compromise. He insisted
> his boyfriend watches that **** or else. He met
> someone new almost straight away.'*

Sanjay, 29, Accountant.

> *'Gay guys are too quick to judge today and dump a
> guy by text or email without a second though for
> superficial reasons like their body or the clothes they
> wear. If they had to dump them in person then they
> would have to think twice or they would maybe even
> make more of an effort to get to know him'.*

Sanjay may have a point; perhaps it is easier to dump
someone using today's means of technology which are
devoid of personal attachment and guilt. But, also, many gay
guys assume that if they have differences with their partner
then the relationship is doomed to fail. This is not always
the case as diversity can be interesting. A couple's

similarities encourage security and comfort but the differences are just as valuable and can bring interest and excitement. But, in Reda's case, above, he is surely better off without a partner who puts more importance on a soap opera than his own boyfriend!

Many guys think that the grass is always greener on the other side of the fence. They are looking for their perfect mate and as soon as they notice the tiniest fault with their current one, they break up and continue with their search. The real, underlying problem here could be either a fear of commitment or, even, an unwillingness to settle down. In some instances, a guy starts mentally nit picking on the first date, just looking for a reason why the relationship could never work; he's too short, he's a bit overweight, etc. This could even be a way of sabotaging relationships, which we will look into more closely later on. If this sounds like something you find yourself doing then try to focus on the positive things about the man you are dating. You will never find perfection as it doesn't exist. If your date has ticked most of your boxes and meets your criteria then think yourself lucky to have met him, especially if he feels the same about you! Do not ruin everything by focusing on one negative point (unless that one point is that he has no teeth or he sleeps with a loaded gun under his pillow.)

The ease of finding new guys to meet on the internet can be a factor which prevents many guys from developing lasting relationships. So if you have had a couple of dates with a nice guy and you feel that there is the possibility of something great developing, then consider not logging into your online dating profile and forget the chat rooms for a while. Give it a chance. Put all your focus on him and not on what or who you could be missing. **The chat room will always be there but this potentially perfect partner won't!**

Jason, 30, Researcher.

> *'I have been seeing Paolo for nearly a month now. I don't want to sleep with anyone else and we both really like each other. The thing is, whenever I go to his place, I notice that he is logged on to his gay chat website and leaves it running on his laptop. Since we met I haven't even logged in to my profile or wanted to search for anyone else. I feel a bit hurt to be honest'.*

Jason gives us a perfect example of how internet dating can get addictive. It may well be that Paolo is crazy about Jason but he is just in the habit of logging into his profile everyday.

It does seem thoughtless and hurtful for him to leave it running on his computer while Jason is visiting him; this is sending out the message that he has not found what he is looking for and is still looking! But, as they have only been seeing each other for a few weeks, Jason does not yet have the right to ask Paolo to turn it off or delete his profile. Unless you have discussed being monogamous or just dating each other exclusively, then everything is still left open at this stage and both parties are still getting to know each other. But, at some stage you both have to stop hunting and give your relationship 100% of your attention. This is also an example of society not yet having come up with rules for new technology such as dating sites; what is the correct etiquette? For the moment; just common sense.

We have seen how having sex too early can give the wrong signals or confuse things. Another risk of having sex on a first date is that if it doesn't go well then many guys don't want to see that guy again. A beautiful relationship can get spoiled due to sexual performance on one occasion.

That perfect, beautiful guy you just met could have been the one but when you slept together he came too fast or had cold feet. No matter how hard you tried to still see him as that perfect guy; you couldn't get over the disappointment. So you didn't call him again.

Sex with a new partner can put pressure on some guys, which is understandable, especially if they are besotted with their partner and trying to make a good impression. Don't make judgements or decisions after the first time you sleep together, especially if you have only known each other a few days or less. Remember that people can *learn* to please one another in bed; there are not always sparks flying on that first encounter.

It's a fact that men are sexual beings who think of sex every few seconds. Some guys put more emphasis on the importance of sex in a relationship than others; it's a very personal choice as the following two opinions illustrate:

James, Solicitor, 30.

> *'I would say that sex is 60% of a relationship. I'm very sexual and it is a big thing for me. If it ain't happening in bed then it ain't happening full stop'.*

Mark, Interior Designer. 28.

> *'You can have amazing sex with someone but that's no good if you have nothing else in common. I want to share my whole life with somebody, not just my bed.'*

If you are looking to enter into a serious, loving relationship then you need to find a way to balance sexual urges and try not to hurry everything. Consider going on a few dates before sleeping together, imagine how the excitement, intimacy and anticipation could grow and create an experience far more fulfilling and satisfying than if you had slept together the first time you had met. Learn to see and respect your date as a human being with many qualities and positive traits before you sleep together, rather than seeing him as a sexual object. Take some time to get a basic understanding of him and get to know him. You could even say something like '*I really like you but I don't sleep with someone on the first couple of dates*' just to make sure he is not looking for a one night stand and to remove any expectation that may be lurking around in the air. Telling someone that you really like them, respect them and want to get to know them before having sex is also a compliment.

The need for instant gratification and allowing yourself to be controlled by your libido can also point to a lack of self confidence. You need patience to get to know a person well and some gay men feel that the object of their desire will not wait around long enough and that they will loose a great sexual opportunity that night! But this really comes down to believing that you are interesting and attractive enough for him to wait around to get to know you because you are a great catch. By the way, remember that you *are* a great catch!

BARRIER No. 2: Not Knowing What You Really Want.

Have you ever looked at the reasons you want to find a partner? Many common responses to that question would be things like: *I want to feel loved, I want to love someone, I want to share my life with someone,* etc. But sometimes the reasons that drive people to start relationships come from outside pressure. Would any of the following apply to you?

> *I'm at the age now where I feel I should settle down with a boyfriend.*

> *All my friends are married or settled down with kids, I'm the only single one left now.*

My mum is constantly nagging me about settling down with someone.

I don't want to end up alone so I'd better start looking now.

I want to spend Christmas with a boyfriend this year instead of alone or with my family.

As we have just seen in the previous chapter, there are no hard and fast rules for gay men; nobody can tell you if you should or should not settle down. If you are happy being single then it is irrelevant that your friends or relations are married with kids etc. It's better to lead a happy single life than start a relationship with the wrong person just because you felt it's what you *should* do at your age. As we've already seen, gay men can have more freedom in relationships that straight people. Gay men can be in a relationship but not live together; there are no assumptions or rules with a gay couple.

Henry, 34, Trader, says:

'Last year my two younger sisters, my straight best friend and my cousin all got married. I attended what seemed like a never ending procession of weddings

throughout the summer. I got lots of comments like 'you're next Henry!' and 'when are you going to get married?' I started to feel a bit anxious about meeting someone and doing the 'normal' thing, settling down and all that. I felt like time was ticking and I was getting older. The more I felt like that, the more impossible it became to meet anyone. Looking back now, I can see that is not really what I wanted. I'm happily single now and staying that way!'

Henry's case shows that outside pressure can make us feel like we should settle down or start a relationship when this is *not* really what we want inside. If you are having trouble trying to find a partner, have you asked yourself if that is *what you really do want?* If you don't like broccoli then your subconscious will automatically steer your trolley away from it in the supermarket without you even noticing. In the same way, if you don't want to be in a relationship then your subconscious will make sure that you sabotage any relationship that comes along without you really understanding what went wrong. Could the reason you are still single be that, in fact, you *want* to be single?

Being single is great. You just have to think of your own wants and needs; you choose where to go on holiday, what you're going to eat for dinner and you don't need to explain yourself to anyone. Many people, both gay and straight, prefer to live like this. Unfortunately, society tends to favour people in couples and pities those who are single. Every single gay man has been to a family wedding or a party and been asked the question '*so how come you're single?*' as if there is something wrong with you. They don't mean this in a bad way, but we live in a culture where people always couple up. If you don't want to, then it just doesn't compute for them. That's why positively affirming that you prefer to remain single can feel guilty or wrong and that is also why many guys unconsciously pretend that they want to find a boyfriend when, underneath, they really don't! You don't need to be in a relationship to have a rich, satisfying, exciting life.

Many gay guys constantly complain that, although they are looking for a partner, they always end up having one night stands and nothing more. If we examine that statement closer, we see that this is a contradiction. If you were seriously looking for a relationship, then one night stands would not be on the agenda. This is another case of feeling you *should* be in a relationship but, in fact, it's not what you really want. On the other hand, if you respond to an online profile where a guy is specifically looking for sex and nothing more, then do not make the mistake of thinking a relationship could develop! I have heard the same story many times from friends and clients who come across a gorgeous guy online or in person, who is just feeling horny, but they go to meet him with other ideas in their head. This could lead to you getting hurt or, even worse, being strung along by someone who just wants sex. If this has happened to you before you need to acknowledge that you were the one in the wrong; the other guy was sending perfectly clear signals regarding what he wanted. Sex is rarely the start of a long-term relationship.

The trick here is to look out for signs that someone is not available for a relationship, move on and stop wasting your time and energy. Here are a few examples of guys who fall into this category:

- Married men.

- Straight guys.

- Guys who are cheating.

- Addicts (sex, drugs, alcohol etc.)

- Guys who are not out, i.e. not comfortable with their sexuality.

- Guys who are clinically depressed.

- Guys who are not over their ex.

You cannot change any of the guys in the above list so don't even try to. You are not their therapist, nor their emotional support, and playing Florence Nightingale will not make him love you. Be firm and start to associate these types of men with flashing red warning lights in your head! If the above reads like a list of your past boyfriends then, hopefully, you have identified the type of unavailable men you keep going for. The next step would be to figure out why you are attracted to men who are not suitable. It may be time to ask yourself some uncomfortable questions. Are you really unavailable for a relationship yourself, deep down? Maybe you want to be single?

If that is the case then what other life ambitions and goals could you focus on until you feel that you do want to start a relationship? Or maybe you will never want to start one and that's fine too. Have fun, be free and respect your decision to be single and resist any pressure from anyone else; especially Auntie Mable at your next family get-together.

Maybe you are sure you want a relationship but you are really not ready for one. If you have not completely come to terms with your sexuality or if you are not 'out', then you are not ready. You really need to be happy with who you are before you can be happy with someone else.   Maybe you have just broken up with someone and you are not really over them? Again, this is not the time to be looking for love. Mourn the end of that relationship and give yourself some time to adjust to being a happy, single person with a fulfilling life rather than going on the rebound.

As we have already seen, there is no model for the typical gay relationship so it's up to you to decide what you want. Do you want to live together or apart? Do you want to have an open relationship? Do you want to see someone on a casual basis or are you looking for the love of your life? This could avoid conflict at a later stage if you chose a partner who is looking for a different kind of relationship. Another important factor is knowing *who* you want. Although that may sound easy, many gay guys have vague ideas about the man they want to be with. By that I don't mean physically (as most gay men could reel off a list of physical attributes, such as tall, gym body, handsome, etc at the drop of a hat), rather, someone that would compliment your personality. Are you looking for someone intellectual or sporty, religious or atheist, a traveller or a home body? Try to work out which qualities would suit you and what kind of person you want to be with and this may help you to make easier choices later on. It's an unfortunate fact that so many gay men put more thought into choosing a new pair of shoes or a holiday destination than choosing a partner.

The best way to figure out what or who you want is to identify your own personality traits and qualities. Make a list of your goals, your good points, your passions and your pastimes. Identify your needs and desires and then the type of man that could meet them will become clearer to you. Perhaps there is a timid side to your personality that would be complimented by someone louder or maybe socialising is a huge part of your life, so you need to be with a very social partner. Spend some time on this; you really have nothing to lose.

BARRIER No. 3: Gay Ideals.

Body Image.

Sex sells. It's used to sell us everything: from pop songs and underwear, to hair colorants and cars. While there has been much recent documentation about magazines and advertising campaigns idealised body images creating

eating disorders among women, gay men have also been affected by the idea of the perfect physique. Adverts showing perfect bodies have become the norm and people think that they too need to have a perfect body to be normal, attractive and acceptable. We have all been to gay clubs which are full of topless muscled torsos and it's easy to see why some argue that many gay men are developing distorted, unhealthy ideas of how they should look. Washboard abs on bill boards and health magazines have trickled down into our everyday existence and this has led gay men to become much more demanding about what they want from a partner. A perfect, worked-out gym body is now the norm among a high percentage of gay men today. As well as a good job, sense of humour etc, gay men want waxed, lasered, tooth bleached and gym-toned Adonises. How many times have you seen that awful phrase: '*No fats, no fems*'written on dating profiles? The attitude which has developed among gay guys today is very much about thinking '*If I spend 3 hours a day in the gym then my partner has to do the same! I won't settle for less!*' There is nothing wrong with taking good care of your physical appearance. The problem starts when gay guys are only interested in other guys who meet a certain physical criteria, for example a muscled body, huge biceps, flat stomach etc. This tunnel vision means they are missing many potential partners who are loving, handsome, compatible and capable of making them very happy, but who do not fit the blueprints for the perfect muscle man embedded in their subconscious. The following quote from a friend of mine illustrates this point:

Jonathan, 27, Solicitor:

> *'I spent my early 20s desperately trying to be part of the gay muscle crowd, at one point I even started taking steroids. I went to the big clubs and took my t shirt off on the dancefloor; I became a bit obsessed. One Saturday night, I took my best girlfriend to one of the big clubs. We were on the dancefloor and I expected her to be blown away by all these super sexy guys, but she leaned over and said 'all these guys look the same, like robots, its freakish.' Over the next 6 months or so I started hanging out with my gay uni friends more, we went to clubs and bars which are more for skinny, young trendy guys, more laid back, and I realised I was having just as much fun with them. I realised my girlfriend was partly right and now I kind of see that I was too focused on my perfect type of man without realising that there are other types out there that are just as sexy'.*

Jonathan's girlfriend gave him a much needed jolt back to reality. It is easy to get carried away by body types and muscles when that is all we see around us. You can't open any gay paper or magazine without seeing images of beefy, gym-toned men. Luckily, he had someone from outside to point this out. Some guys don't and they stay stuck in a very fixed viewpoint of what is attractive.

Being realistic about yourself and your looks is paramount; you are more likely to attract the man of your dreams if you take care of your appearance and hygiene but, on the other hand, do not become so wrapped up in your idea of your dream man that you are blinded and end up missing the perfect guy who was right in front of you, but you didn't notice him as his biceps weren't big enough, he was too hairy or too smooth. If this is ringing bells for you, go back to basics and examine what you are really looking for; arm candy that looks great or compatibility, conversation and companionship that will last. Of course sexual attraction is important, in fact, it's vital! Without it, the human race would probably disappear! It's what attracts us to other guys in the first place and, as we saw in the last chapter, it is an important part of a relationship, but not as important as marketing and advertising directors would like us to believe. We will see later how many men get stuck in patterns of going for the same thing again and again and it's wise to try to find out the reasons behind this behaviour. Try to separate your sex drive and your emotional desire for a relationship, we all know this is not easy and we are all human, but in the long-term (and that's what anyone looking for a stable relationship is looking towards) the perfect muscle body becomes harder to maintain and Gucci jeans don't look so amazing when you are 60 compared to when you were 25.

Yanis, Student, 32:

> *I think it's important to remember that physical beauty fades with familiarity. Over time you no longer have the same 'wow' factor to your boyfriend's biceps, etc. You see him everyday so you develop a picture of him based on emotions and all the good things about his personality.'*

Yanis' wise words remind us how emotional, intellectual and spiritual connections outlast physical attraction.

Masculinity.

Let's go back to that overused phrase which can be seen on many online profiles: 'no fats or fems'. Masculinity is attractive. We are men attracted to men; that makes sense, right? It is also a gay ideal. As we've already seen, our culture says femininity is not very acceptable among men. Whether straight or gay, we should be strong, breadwinning cavemen who don't show our feelings. Emotions, dependence and, shock horror, homosexuality is wrong wrong wrong. So it's no wonder that gay men try to escape their feminine side. Many school boys repress themselves to distract attention from their sexual preferences or behaviour which could result in bullying. If not addressed, this behaviour tends to remain with them throughout their life. The goal of many gay men is to appear on the surface to be 'straight acting'. Many guys take this to extremes by developing hyper masculine bodies using steroids and constantly monitoring the way they talk, walk and act. This is indeed a 'straight act' but based on what or who? Arnie Schwarzenegger in Terminator or the typical image of a gun toting cowboy from a 50s Western film, devoid of expression and emotion, are outdated and inaccurate. We live in an age of equality and communication where straight men can take paternity leave to bring up their baby while their wife is working and young generations of straight men today think nothing of using facial moisturiser, lip balm and hair straighteners. So, who are these gay guys trying to mimic? An image in their imagination or a former teacher or a male relation who made a big impression on their development, perhaps? All men, whether gay or straight, posses a range of characteristics, qualities and traits which are both masculine and feminine. Imagine a scale of one to ten. A macho, butch guy who is on the scale at number one somehow does not seem natural; there is something not quite right about him. He is trying too hard. On the other end of the scale, is an outrageously camp guy at number 10, he also seems to be putting on a big act. We are all somewhere between these two extremes and wherever we are on the scale is perfectly fine and natural. The hugest body builder in your local gym may well cry like a baby when watching a sad film and, on the other hand, that attention-grabbing, camp hairdresser who cuts your hair could actually be straight! Trying to be somebody else is tiring and time consuming. Life is short and there is too much fun to be had. Tyler points out how you can't fool people by trying to be someone else:

Tyler, Student, 24.

> *'Sometimes I see a really huge, beefy guy in a club and think; wow he is so sexy and masculine but then he opens his mouth and he is the campest guy ever'. His image just doesn't match the person.'*

Many gay guys celebrate their femininity and think nothing of donning a pink wig at the drop of a hat or singing to Britney at Friday night's karaoke. Instead of practicing walking like a cowboy, they practice Beyoncé's latest dance routine. These guys are often the subject of ridicule from other 'straight acting' gay guys. They can't stand this camp behaviour. What we all need to remember at times is that what we hate in others is what we hate in ourselves. Many guys have not yet fully accepted the feminine part of their character, which makes them who they are. Secondly, these kinds of comments and derision are often driven by internalised homophobia which has been absorbed throughout a lifetime of being rejected and marginalised by straight society. Nobody is saying you have to go to extremes and put on the wig but you do need to feel comfortable with who you are. It's fine to be turned off by the guy dancing to Beyoncé, but to others this could be a huge turn on.

Human sexuality is very complex. Some gay guys (as well as bi and straight men and women) are attracted to feminine guys. There is no need to change who you are or how you act as you think that it's not attractive. There is someone for everyone; four years of watching speed dating events has taught me that! A tall, handsome man will sometimes get less date requests at the end of the night than a shorter, less traditionally beautiful guy who has a great sense of humour and is very confident. Accepting the feminine part of other gay guys and not disliking them for it (it's just a small part of a person's whole personality, not a reason to avoid knowing them) may even open new doors and relationship possibilities for you.

Hervé, Stylist, 28

> *'After years and years of hating being gay and who I really was, I have come to love the feminine side of my personality because without it I wouldn't have such a great understanding of fashion, fabrics and dressing a woman's body.'*

Hervé gives us a perfect example of accepting and loving yourself. Many gay guys are sensitive, artistic or creative and succeed in many specific industries (such as fashion design, hairdressing, nursing or caring) due to their sexuality. Being gay can make men more caring, sensitive and understanding than if they had been born straight. So try to see these positive points in your own personality. Try to be thankful for your sexuality and who you are. You have no choice but to live with your sexuality so you may as well start to love and accept it now.

Now, let's look at the other side of the coin. What would you consider as outward signs of masculinity? Facial stubble or, perhaps, a hairy chest? So, if gay men are attracted to masculinity then how come so many gay guys (I stress *some*, not all) pluck their eyebrows to oblivion, wear very obvious make-up, wax every single strand of body hair from the neck down and aim for a size zero waist, etc. It seems they want to obliterate any last trace of masculinity from their appearance. Of course, everyone is free to express themselves as they like and wear what makes them feel comfortable and I am certainly not telling anyone how they should dress but, doesn't this seem to be counter-productive? If a gay man likes masculinity and wants to attract that very quality, then why are so many gay guys uncomfortable with expressing it? My theory (hold on to your hats) is that this goes back to childhood. Many gay boys love spending time with their sisters or female friends and they feel very comfortable in a feminine, girly environment. At a certain age, parents often step in and say something along the lines of '*OK, enough's enough! Now it's time for you to start playing football with the boys'.* The child may, unwillingly, be sent to a football club or something equally boyish in the hope that he will let go of his attachment to dolls or anything connected to girls. Even if this push doesn't come from his parents, it will certainly come from his school; boys and girls are separated. The response from this young boy/ adolescent, who is being forced into a mould, which he does not feel comfortable with, is rebellion. He goes against what his parents/ school/ society expect from him and he acts in a feminine way. He deliberately, or unconsciously, develops feminine ways of acting or speaking. His football boots are tossed aside as he chooses clothes and hairstyles which look feminine and will make his peers, parents and teachers notice. He aims to shock, to horrify and to go against the grain. By the time he is in his late teens, this rebellion could mean he is outrageously camp and militantly gay and this could well go on for the rest of his life. However, as a mature adult, he needs to realise that he is free to live as he pleases and there is nobody to rebel against. He is now free to follow his own path to masculinity, whether this means being very close to girls or going out into the gay community and realising those hair styles aren't nearly as shocking as he thinks. It's OK to be masculine and gay at the same time and the link between his homosexuality and feminine or camp behaviour can be broken. As we saw earlier, sexual attraction is a hugely complex issue but a man who is comfortable with his own masculinity (as well as his femininity) is surely more attractive to others. There is no need to put on a 'straight act' but, at the same time, there is no need to rebel or try to shock. A friend of mine illustrates my point:

Youssef, 34, Graphic Designer:

'I come from a very strict, male dominated, Arab country and from quite an early age I wanted to dye my hair pink and do things that shocked my parents and neighbours and everyone around me. When I moved to London, I was 22 years old and I realised that there were gay men who looked like regular, manly, straight men. I realised that I could drop the whole pink hair thing! I could be gay without constantly putting so much emphasis into projecting a feminine image. It was a revelation but also a relief.'

Thankfully, many gay guys make this connection as they are growing up and have no further issues but, for others, this can hinder their relationships and their efforts to find a partner. Judging by the multitude of gay men who write *'no fats, no fems'* or *'not into camp guys'* on their online profiles, we could assume that a gay man who is outrageously camp is limiting his opportunities and excluding many potential dates. If he is happy in himself and does not see that as an issue then its fine; those picky guys don't know what they're missing! As we saw earlier, accepting the feminine side of our character is healthy and good. On the other hand, if he does see this as a problem then, possibly, he may want to think about what drives his behaviour. Is there some over-compensation, some insecurity that leads to putting on an act or is that rebellious teenager inside still throwing a tantrum?

The fixed image of a perfect man does not necessarily have to be build around body shape or masculinity; it could also be focused on wealth. Some guys are only interested in meeting rich men. Other guys are focused only on men from a certain social class or education. Many online profiles read: *I am looking for Latino or black guys only*. If that's what floats your boat, no problem! But, many guys are being so specific about what they want that they are making finding a relationship very hard for themselves. They are casting their net wide but letting most of the fish through the net! Don't confuse sexual attraction with the desire for a long lasting relationship. The qualities that matter in the long run are compatibility, respect, companionship and honesty. It may be the case that the image you have of your Mr Perfect is so precise and impossible to achieve for a reason. Maybe, underneath, you want to remain single as we discussed in the last section on knowing what you want. I would like to finish this section with a couple of views from my clients:

Gerard, 43, Web Developer.

> *'There is a gay obsession with the perfect body and all that and because of this there's more exclusion. Groups of gay guys tend to reflect a similarity be it in friendships or partnerships. If you go for one type only, you are missing out! You've cut your odds of winning - you'll lose unless you're lucky'.*

Jamie, Student, 26.

> *'I don't like the way that the gay world is based on guys with gym bodies. But if I look at a guy who's got an amazing body then sometimes I think to myself that he would not be interested in me as I'm not as fit as him. But that means that I am being really superficial and reducing everything on physical appearance, which is just as bad'.*

BARRIER No. 4: Low Self Esteem:

Today's younger generation will grow up seeing gay
politicians and gay TV presenters regularly and gay children
will be able to identify with some positive role models. But,
children from older generations or other cultures are not so
lucky. As we saw in chapter one, gay men can have difficult
childhoods. From a very early age, young children absorb
what is around them. This includes the attitudes and beliefs
of their parents and family; children sense when their
parents are uncomfortable or upset about something. Our
macho culture and most religions reject homosexuality as
wrong and bad. Through the years, gay children internalise
this homophobia and, by the time they are young adults, can
end up believing that they are bad and unworthy. Many gay
children suffer from bullying at school, which causes
withdrawal and feelings of inferiority. When they finally do
come out, they can face more rejection from their friends
and family. A child who has not received parental love and
support can grow up to believe they do not deserve to be
loved or to be happy. They can often end up sabotaging
perfect relationships because of this, without being aware
they are doing it.

In adulthood, this inferiority and insecurity can manifest anywhere between the following two extremes. The first is the gay guy who wants to hide himself away to protect himself from criticism or aggression. He doesn't believe anyone could love him and has a huge lack of self esteem and confidence. He settles for too little with his career and life in general. At the other end of the scale is the gay guy who overcompensates. During his childhood, he did not receive the love he needed so he now turns to material possessions for comfort instead of loving relationships. He has excelled in his career and is obsessed by having the most expensive car on the street, the biggest biceps in the gym. He is over compensating for his lack of self-esteem. This type of guy is often loud, attention grabbing, bitchy, showy and always dressed in designer labels. He is seeking prestige and admiration. The following quote gives us a good example of this kind of behaviour and shows it can have other causes too;

Marcel, 38, Marketing Assistant says:

> *'When I first arrived from Brazil, I hardly spoke English at all. I used to feel so stupid when I was trying to buy something in a shop or explain something to someone, like everyone was laughing at*

me. I also had this thing in my head that I was shorter than English people and that made me embarrassed as well. I suppose I reacted by being really arrogant; the way I walked and treated people. I used to strut around like a real diva! Now I feel really embarrassed about what I used to do.'

Hmm, guys strutting around like real divas; does that ring any bells? Unfortunately, we all know that this second type of attention grabbing personality is everywhere on the gay scene. Years of hate, which have come from his own culture or religion or the people around him in his childhood, have been directed internally and are often expressed by being bitchy about other gay people (insulting others and putting other gay guys down to make themselves feel better and superior.) It is a sad fact that the atmosphere in many gay bars and clubs is often bitchy and full of 'attitude', which makes it even more difficult for our marginal group to meet each other and start relationships and friendships. If you think you have issues from your childhood then you probably know that these have to be resolved before you can move forward with your life and find that ever elusive perfect relationship. We all deserve to be loved and we should all respect ourselves and each other. Although many guys put off therapy or counselling to resolve past issues because they know it will open a Pandora's box of problems which they don' t want to face (and it's much easier to turn to drugs or alcohol in the short term) there will come a time when this is necessary.

Of course, in between these two extremes are gay guys who are confident, balanced, happy and successful in all parts of their lives apart from their sexuality. They could give a confident work presentation to a thousand people but become tongue-tied and shy when it comes to dating and meeting guys.

Another symptom of insecurity is jealousy. While the green eyed monster is normal in small doses, it has wrecked many a gay relationship due to one partner feeling threatened by other men. He often feels inferior or scared of someone stealing his man away and reacts with anger. I recently was out in a bar with a good friend and his partner and another guy walked up to us, said it was his birthday and wanted my friend to give him a happy birthday kiss. My friend gave him a grandmotherly peck on the cheek, it couldn't have been more loveless, but it was enough to send his partner into a fit of jealousy. The night (and eventually the relationship) was ruined. Anyone who witnessed the event could clearly see that he was the one with the issue. Jealousy is just another way for insecurity to rear its ugly head.

The bottom line is overcoming fear; fear of being alone, fear of being rejected, fear of being abandoned, fear of being cheated on, etc. Trying to link your behavioural patterns with your upbringing can bring instant understanding, relief and compassion. Again, if you do not want to see a therapist, there are plenty of self-help books (such as this one) which can help you gain understanding and improve your chances of finding (and keeping) love.

Some guys are naturally shy (and this has nothing to do with their sexuality or inferiority complexes), especially when they are new to the gay scene, and there is nothing wrong with that; in fact, shyness is an endearing quality to posses. What can happen is that they try to be something they are not to compensate for their lack of confidence; some guys turn on a super camp persona when they go out, which is a million miles away from who they are during the day. Others try to model themselves on someone else, erroneously thinking that this will make them more attractive. The problem is that when these pretenders do meet someone they like, they have to carry on this needless act the whole time, which can be exhausting. Take Christina Aguilera's advice; you are beautiful! Be yourself and realise that you are a unique, fantastic person with great qualities and leave the acting to the professionals. Imagine how boring the world would be if everyone had the same personality?

Body Language; that old chestnut again.

During the last four years or so I have seen many guys lacking self confidence at the dating events I run. Their biggest mistake is their body language (are you bored of hearing about this yet? Good! I know this keeps coming up but it cannot be stressed enough.) Their insecurity makes them cross their legs or fold their arms, which creates a barrier between them and their date. This automatically gives the impression that they are not interested when often the reality is the complete opposite! The second mistake is to avoid eye contact; focusing on the floor, fiddling with a pen or looking anywhere but in the direction of your date's face gives a disinterested impression and may even be misconstrued as rudeness or arrogance. Nobody would expect you to stare into your date's eyes constantly the whole time (this could well freak him out) but you need to make sure you are looking deep into his eyes every now and then to show interest. If you feel too shy to look into someone's eyes then try to focus on the area around their forehead and eyebrows, it has the same affect. Posture is another important aspect. Walking tall with your shoulders and back straight gives an air of confidence, even when you don't feel it; this is attractive. Slouching and sitting hunched over, resting on your elbows makes you look smaller, bored and lethargic.

The last thing I want you to do is spend the whole date obsessing over his (or your own) body language and what it might mean. You are there to have fun and need to concentrate on making conversation and getting to know each other. Use the following chart as a general guide to judge if he is interested or not but don't make any conclusions after he crosses his arms once; consider his body language during the whole evening rather than one or two specific actions and don't get too analytical. Although many will consider all these little actions easy to avoid, after all its just common sense, body language doesn't lie! You can't fake or hide it (unless you're an Oscar winning actor.) The following hints should help you to learn some basic signs to watch out for:

GOOD SIGNS:

Pointing his glass, elbow, knee or anything else towards you: (but not his finger or, worse, a gun!): this means he is interested in you!

Mirroring your movements:
he is definitely interested.

Preening behaviour:
straightening his back, pushing out his chest and pulling in his stomach: he wants to impress you.

Trying to look manlier:
Hands resting on his belt, fingers pointing to his crotch or standing with his legs apart. If he is seated, stretching out to make himself look bigger. It means he wants to attract your attention.

Blocking other guys from seeing or approaching you.
He wants you for himself.

Leaning forward in his seat toward you. He is eager to hear more.

BAD SIGNS:

Touching his nose or eye while speaking: he's lying.

Leaning away from you or looking away: he's not interested.

Folding his arms and/ or crossing his legs: he is not interested; he's put up a barrier.

Looking around the room while you're speaking: he's bored or, worse, he's looking for someone else!

Avoiding eye contact: not interested/ something to hide.

NEUTRAL SIGNS

Playing with his hair: he lacks confidence.

Stroking his chin: he is trying to make a decision.

Pulling at his earlobe: he is undecided.

Apart from body language, guys lacking in confidence need to work on feeling better about themselves inside. There are hundreds of books you can read to build your self confidence; I would like you to take just five minutes a day to try the following exercise. The idea is to reframe the way you see and think about yourself. After one week, I guarantee you will feel more confident and happy about yourself, but you have to do this every day. Take a pen and list all the great skills and qualities you posses. This could be looks, abilities, achievements or anything else you can think of, at least 10 or 15 lines per day. Be specific and don't write generalisations like 'I am nice'. Here is an example:

I am really friendly.

I am clever, I have a degree.

I love helping people.

I am good at maths.

I have good dress sense.

I speak good French.

I have a great body.

I am a loving person.

When you think about all the great qualities, skills and traits you have it really is not so hard to make this list. Start now on the following page. Grab a pen and start writing now.

....

....

....

....

....

....

....

....

....

....

....

....

As you go through the week you will see how this list grows and grows and you will see how the more thought you give this, the more interesting, fantastic things you can state about yourself. The idea is that after a week of making a new list every day, the way you feel about yourself will start to change. After one week you could repeat the exercise for a second or even third week. Hopefully, you will feel more positive about who you are and what you have to offer your future partner or even the world!

Look over this list before you go on a date and keep these positive qualities in your head. We can only think one thought at a time so whenever an insecure thought comes into your head (i.e. I'm overweight, my hair is a mess) replace it immediately with all the wonderful things on your list. Remember that your date is lucky to be spending time with a person who has so much to give!

As well as feeling good on the inside, perhaps there are things you could improve about your image that would make you feel more self confident and happier with yourself.

- If you are unhappy with your body shape, join a gym (which is a great way to meet new people too.)

- I have met many tall guys who are self conscious and develop bad posture as they try to make themselves look shorter. Pilates and yoga are excellent for improving posture and making you walk and look more confident.

- Some guys become very self conscious when they start to loose their hair. The shaved-head look is very fashionable now. If that's not your style, you could look into hair replacement technology.

- Ask an honest friend or even a stranger how they see your style. Do you dress your age? Do your clothes and hairstyle look dated? What impression do your clothes give? Conservative, stuffy, trendy or contemporary? Be ready for an image change if necessary, this will do wonders for your self-confidence.

- Remember that many gay guys have fetishes or specific interests in all body types and looks from bears and tall guys to cubs (young bears) and redheads. You are sure to be somebody's cup of tea!

I have spoken with many gay guys at my events who have complained of feeling lonely but they have just given up trying to do something about it. Sometimes they have suffered so much rejection that they don't have the confidence to date anymore. Others never had much self esteem to begin with and had problems meeting men from the start. For whatever reason, they end up sitting at home; alone and feeling sorry for themselves rather than trying to meet their match. We discussed many ways that guys can join social groups etc to meet new gay guys for friendship and dating, but, as well as doing that, I would advise getting out there and building an interesting, fulfilling life for yourself before you start looking for a mate. You will have much more to offer and be a more interesting, happier person to be with and, on top of that, you will be in a far better place to handle the ups and downs of a relationship if it's not the main focus in your life. Forget meeting guys for a moment and force yourself to get out of the house for a couple of nights a week just to do something social with other people (straight or gay.) Study something or start a new sport. Practise socialising, building friendships and new interests. Some guys are chronically shy or introverted so it may be the case that you need to take this step by step; that's fine. The main thing is to get out there and enjoy your life. Having a boyfriend should be just the cherry on top of an already rich, fruity, delicious cake!

The worse mistake that shy or insecure guys can make is thinking that alcohol or drugs can give them confidence. The effects of whisky, cocaine or any other type of drug are temporary and don't fool anyone. Some people *feel* more confident inside after a couple of drinks but to the outside world they just look drunk. What happens when the high wears off? If you feel you need a confidence boost from drugs or alcohol then it's time to look at your self-esteem and maybe even ask yourself if you have an addiction?

BARRIER No. 5: Desperation!

Remember Charlotte on Sex and the City when she freaked out because her boyfriend hadn't proposed to her yet? They were just sitting at home and she suddenly started yelling at him to SET THE DATE, SET THE DATE!! The result was that he broke up with her (although he had already bought a ring and was planning on asking her.) That's an extreme example, but guys can occasionally become so obsessed with finding their Mr Right that they don't realise they are coming across like Charlotte.

Mick, 31, Architect:

'I had just one date with a great guy who I really liked. On the way back home after the date he texted me twice, which I thought was sweet. But the next day he texted me 6 times just in the morning He wrote stuff like 'I can see we are perfect for each other' and 'do you want to come to my sisters house next week'. His good looks and the good impression he made at dinner went out the window 'cause he was just so desperate. It was a total turn-off for me, I felt suffocated. I don't wanna sound harsh but that first time you meet someone is when you need to make a good impression. I didn't see him again.'

Sending a text to thank your date for dinner is fine. But, as Mick points out, being hounded by texts can feel invasive and annoying. Even if you are convinced on your first date that you are sitting opposite your Mr Dreamboat, coming across as too eager could easily turn the whole thing into a shipwreck. If you do find yourself feeling like Charlotte, try to give the impression you are more like Miranda; cool and calm.

Having a stable relationship is a wonderfully rewarding and worthwhile thing but remember that there is more to life than that. If you feel you could be coming across as too desperate maybe you are trying to hard? Maybe you think a relationship will make your life perfect, but are you really trying to distract yourself from parts of your life which are far from perfect? Meeting Mr Right will not fix a bad relationship with your parents, make any difference to an unsatisfying job or the fact that you are unhappy with your body. Imagine your life as a big pie (or maybe a quiche for the healthy eaters out there) divided up into sections. One quarter could be labelled 'my career', one quarter could be labelled 'my hobbies and interests' and one quarter (or third or half, its up to you to assign how important each section is to you) could be labelled 'my relationship'. The idea is that you should be seeing your life as balanced and fulfilled rather than waiting for a relationship to come along and make everything better like some miracle cure.

We also need to remember that when we are dating someone new, everyone has their own time frame. Some guys will feel like planning the wedding after the first couple of dates while others never let their heart control their head and take things at a much slower pace. The faster paced guy may well think the other guy is not interested when that is not the case. He also has to make sure his intensity does not scare his mate away. This is different from coming across as too desperate but it is something to bear in mind if you are the passionate type.

BARRIER No. 6: The Single Syndrome.

Many gay men who have been single for a long time (a few years or so) get used to the idea of living alone; they don't feel desperate about meeting the right guy. They create a comfortable home, great friends and a fulfilling life. If they are dating someone and it doesn't work out, that's fine. They have created a great life to fall back on and there is no urgency. Mr Single Syndrome will often say things like 'I've tried dating, but I never find the right type of guy' or 'nobody comes anywhere near to my standards'. This type of 'been there, done that' attitude will do nothing to help him find a partner. He has come to love his perfectly organised, materially comfortable life but he is in a dating rut. What he could try is to take a step outside his comfortable life and try new approaches to thinking about who and what he wants. Although he has been searching for a long time, there is always something new; has he tried joining a gay sports group, a gay cruise, a gay wine tasting group or something slightly out of the norm which will take him out of his attitude of apathy and lethargy? Secondly, after all these years of dating, if he is still saying things like 'nobody comes up to my standards' then maybe it's time to re-examine these standards and see how they could possibly be holding him back? Maybe you can identify with this tiresome search for Mr Right and you feel you have had enough dates to last a lifetime. If so, you are probably giving a tired, dull impression and now is the time to put some passion and energy back into your whole dating 'routine'. Shake things up! Make it more enjoyable! It is supposed to be fun meeting new guys and getting to know them so chose an unusual place to meet (in the zoo, in an unusual art exhibition, on top of a landmark building- be creative), talk about things which motivate you and make you feel great. Talk about things you enjoy and convey that interest. Inject some enthusiasm! You will come across as interesting, vital and enthusiastic, which could change your dating results.

Over time, Mr Single Syndrome's idea of his perfect mate gets more and more specific and that's natural. But time is always ticking. As we get older we learn more about life and ourselves; what we want and what we don't want. The things we could have accepted in a partner when we were 21 (untidy, heavy smoker, poor, no ambition) are drastically reduced by the age of 40. We become less flexible and take fewer chances. Think of some of the people you dated when you were in your teens or early twenties. Are they the type of guys you would still date today? Back then you may have been happy to date a penniless student or a rock singer who was up all night. Today you can't stay up late every night as you have to work and you expect a certain level of comfort in your life; you want to enjoy good food rather than eating in fast food joints.

This quote is from a friend of mine who was telling me what his mother just said to him:

> *'Do you think I would marry your father if I met him now? After all that life has taught me? Of course not!'*

Presumably, she said this after a row with her husband! What she meant is that what she wanted when she was a young twenty something has totally altered compared to what she would want now if she was looking for a mate. But she understands that now, although she has the wisdom, she doesn't have the same looks so it would be very difficult to find all these qualities in a man. She would have to settle for second best. She understands that she took her chance when she was younger and more flexible. But many people do not understand this and they stay single into their 30s or

40s waiting for the impossible. They are happy with their life but they also have very fixed ideas on who they are looking for. This is the single syndrome; if you didn't settle down during that free and easy, 'take a chance' period of life and you are still searching this could be your barrier. Guys that are so happy with their single lives that they would kick Brad Pitt out of bed if he started smoking a cigarette in their non-smoking home. While they stay single and out of a relationship, waiting for Mr Right, they are loosing touch with how relationships work, how both partners need to compromise and give and take. Perfection really does not exist, (even those Abercrombie and Fitch models probably cut there toenails in bed and suffer from bad breath) so gay guys who are waiting on the platform for the train to Perfect Town are going to have a long, long wait. Take Carrie, the fictional character from Sex and The City; she has great friends, a great job and although she is looking for the man of her dreams, she has the excitement of a constant stream of dates with good looking, eligible bachelors. She shops for new outfits and shoes so she always looks great at the most glamorous bars and restaurants in Manhattan. Her life is great and it's easy to see why many people get addicted to this kind of lifestyle. Gay men have it even better because they don't have to worry about having children before its too late.

Guys who have been dating and looking for love for many years sometimes become jaded. They have suffered a broken heart too many times to remember so they build a wall around their heart to protect themselves from getting hurt again. They know that if they don't get in too deep then it will be easy to press the 'emergency stop' button at any time and they can go back to their comfortable single life. Any gardener who loves roses knows that in order to cultivate the most beautiful flowers you will need to get pricked by a few thorns every now and then. The gardener doesn't give up his passion because of this fear, nor does he try gardening wearing a suit of armour for protection; that just wouldn't work. Being successful in the dating game means we have to be vulnerable; being cold and hard just doesn't work.

If you think the singe syndrome could be your barrier to finding a successful relationship then the first stage is to acknowledge this! Maybe you feel your life is so complete being single that you don't need a partner. That is a perfectly acceptable decision to make. But, if you do not feel that way then you need to step back into the dating ring again. Re-examine your wants and needs regarding your ideal mate. Have they been holding you back? Are they realistic? If you are ten stone overweight with no teeth but you insist on your partner being a young male model or if you have been single for quite a few years then the response could be yes. Examine how your attitudes have changed over the years and look at the long list of things you are expecting and the long list of things you will not put up with. Try to shorten both these lists, be hard on yourself. Think about some of the people you know who are in stable relationships, watch them together and see how there is constant compromise. Nobody is getting their way all the time, it's a two way street. Learning to be more flexible is the key to finding your mate.

BARIER No.7: Game Playing:

Men, gay or straight, are the traditional hunters; they are looking for challenge and conquest. Straight men enjoy pursuing women; it's an exciting game and they feel rewarded when they catch her. This primordial impulse also applies to many gay men who love the thrill of the chase. Making yourself too available by cancelling your own plans to see him, telling him how much you like him all the time, in short bending over backwards to make him happy can give the signal that the game is over and he's won. The conquest is completed and now he needs a new challenge and a new man. Being too available can be a turn off as some guys are looking for a challenge; they want to fight for you. If it's a walk over then they loose interest, as Gareth points out:

Gareth, 34, Accountant.

> *'If a guy agrees to meet me whenever I call him and I know I can decide where and when then after a while it's a bit of a turn-off as it seems he is sitting there waiting for my call and desperate to see me so he can't have much of a life'.*

Although not all men are the same, this pattern is played out many times a day in the gay community. You could try holding back a little to keep him interested but, in the long run, if you have met someone who is always looking for the next challenge, then sustaining his interest during a long-term relationship will prove difficult if not impossible. With straight women, the game is over when she gets married to the guy. Check out your local bookstore and you will see shelves full of books for straight women with titles like *Treat him mean to keep him keen* or *Be a bitch to win your man*. With gay men, it is not so clear and trying to not look too keen and playing games can get confusing and even backfire, as the following story shows:

Jason and Christian spent a great evening together on their first date. They found they had so much in common, they were compatible in so many ways and they were both hugely attracted to each other. Christian said he would call Jason in a couple of days to arrange something for the weekend, they kissed and said goodbye.

Although Christian was crazy about Jason, he waited a week before calling him, as he didn't want to come across as too keen.

When Jason saw Christian's number flash up on his phone he didn't answer. He wanted Christian to think he was busy with his fabulous job and not thinking about him, when in fact this was all he had been thinking of the whole week. Christian called a second time that evening and left a voicemail but assumed Jason wasn't interested.

Jason wanted to come across as cool and not too eager so he waited two days before returning Christians call. Christian saw Jason calling and hung up. He was over Jason and had already started dating someone new.

This story is to illustrate how playing games to give a certain impression to your date can become complex and sometimes end in disaster. In this case, if Christian and

Jason had just been honest then they could have already been on two or three more great dates together.

We've all been there, you receive a long awaited text from the object of your desire and just as you are about to instantly reply, a well meaning friend pipes up *'no, don't reply straight away, he'll think you're too keen! Wait a day, he'll want you more'.* He sent you the text because he is interested in you so waiting an hour or day will not change that interest. Only you can judge whether playing games is worth the risk of loosing your date's interest.

It can be confusing and frustrating too, when your love interest takes days to answer a message and keeps you hanging on with anticipation. Do you really want to be with someone who is giving you confusing signals? Does he not respond to your texts because he is not really interested, too busy, playing hard to get or is he just being lazy? You deserve better than any of these reasons so the best thing may be to move on. Life is complicated enough without games and miscommunication in our love lives!

Do not make the mistake of reading the signs wrong. If he is not responding to your texts or making any effort to see you then he is probably not interested in you. Don't always assume he is playing games or playing hard to get. Ask a good friend for advice as we sometimes need an outsider to help us see the reality of what is happening under our own nose. It's difficult when we become so involved with someone we like. Jack explains this point perfectly:

Jack, 33, Sales Manager.

> 'After one month of seeing this guy, I was still not sure if he liked me or not. He never used to invite me round to his place; I always had to invite myself. He never once came to mine or suggested we go out for dinner or anything like that. He never really asked about my life or wanted to know about me either. He never called me, I always texted or called him. But when we were alone I felt it was great and he was loving and sexy. My best friend told me to wake up and smell the coffee; this guy obviously was not into me in the slightest. I needed someone to slap me in the face and wake me up'.

Many of us can relate to Jacks story. No matter how many years of dating experience we have, sometimes our heart controls our head. This is also a perfect example of the importance of good friends! Leave the games for the kids (and straight people) and go find your man.

BARRIER No. 8: I Should Be So Lucky in Love...

If you have been single for quite a few years and your dates never lead anywhere you may well find yourself bemoaning the situation to your friends, saying things like;

> *All the gay guys out there are crazy or weird! I keep meeting the worst kind!*

> *Gay guys just want sex! Nobody wants anything serious!*

> *I am perfect boyfriend material but none of the guys I've dated so far saw it!*

> *I'm the unluckiest person in the world when it comes to love!*

So, are all the guys out there crazy, just looking for sex, etc or are you just trying to blame everyone else for the fact that you have been unable to meet a suitable partner? Who can blame you? It's far easier to sit back and accuse the world around you of failing you rather than looking at yourself and seeing how you could change the situation or change your behaviour. Maybe one or more of the issues we have looked at so far apply to you. List the last ten guys who you dated and why each relationship did not work out. It is very unlikely that each of these ten relationships did not work solely because of the other guy. You were there too! It takes two to tango and you are partly responsible for any relationship in your life. Blaming him is an easy option but it won't help you understand yourself or get what you want in the long run.

The other important thing to note about the above phrases you are repeating to your friends is that they are so negative. We get what we think about. Everyone has (or has had) an old auntie or some old relation who is constantly moaning about how bad his or her health is. People are scared to ask them how they are because they receive a depressing list of ailments from arthritis, back pain to indigestion and how unbearable their suffering is. These type of people love the attention they get from their audience, they love playing the victim and get addicted to the sympathy they receive. Their focus is only on their suffering. They never talk about anything else or imagine that they could ever feel better or be cured and so that is how they stay. Thinking and talking about being ill equals being ill. Thinking and talking about feeling great equals feeling great. So, if you are moping around telling everyone you know how it's impossible to find a partner, then, guess what? You *will* stay single, feeling frustrated, disappointed and unfulfilled and it *will be* impossible to find a partner.

If you recognise the above phrases as something you regularly think or say, imagine the effect of these words on those around you. Nobody wants to be with somebody negative who will bring them down, as a friend or as a partner. Replace: *It's impossible to find a boyfriend* with *I can't wait till I meet my Mr Right* or *I know my boyfriend will come along at the right time.* The effects of this positive thinking are life changing. Firstly, you are making yourself feel better and that will make you more attractive as a person. We all love to be with happy, positive people! They lift us up and make us feel good; we want to be around them. Telling someone *'I'm sick of looking for love, it's too hard'* will provoke a reaction in the listener of *'oh, how depressing, I'd better get away from him'.* But, saying *'I'm on the look out for my perfect guy'* may well encourage the listener to think about any single gay friends they have. You never know... Secondly, you are changing your energy from negative to positive; like attracts like, its physics! Remember all those experiments you did in the science lab back at school? Positive things attract positive things and it's the same with people. Your positive attitude, energy, thoughts and words will bring along your partner. He will come flying into your life like a paperclip drawn to a big magnet. Try it and see; you have nothing to lose (except that big frown.) But when he arrives you have to be aware of your responsibility to make things work. You can not blame him for everything.

A friend who recently split up with a guy he had been seeing for two months told me recently:

> *'Can you believe it; he even invited me to a Mexican restaurant. You know how much I hate spicy food'*

> I replied: *'Yea, but does he know that?'*

> *'What, I have to tell him everything? If he was a proper boyfriend and really cared about me he would have asked me. It's not for me to tell him everything.'*

I immediately realised I had a perfect quote for this book; an example of not taking responsibility. His boyfriend is not a mind-reader. My friend has to tell his boyfriend what he wants and stop playing the victim. Communication is essential in any relationship or friendship.

BARRIER No. 9: Repeating the Same Old Patterns.

We all know the tragic, self destructive example of the battered housewife. When she finally does escape her violent husband, she runs into the arms of another violent man and the whole cycle begins again. She subconsciously chooses a man with the same traits without realising it and she ends up being unhappy and not understanding how the same thing could have happened again (and sometimes again and again.) This is an extreme example, but many gay guys keep going for the same type of guys again and again. They know inside somewhere that the relationship is not suitable and it will not work out but they still dive right in.

Peter, 45, Architect.

'I had a stormy relationship with a young 22 year old Brazilian guy when I was 35. He was too young and we had hardly anything in common. There was a language and cultural barrier but for some reason we stayed together for almost 6 months. When it ended, I found myself looking out for the same type of young Brazilian guy and I found him. Again, this second relationship didn't work out but, amazingly, I didn't see the pattern and I kept on going out with these

young Brazilian guys and ending up unhappy! It took
a friend to point out the obvious cycle. I'm sure a
therapist would tell me what the underlying problem
was, all I know is that I want to be happy, not
constantly frustrated .'

Peter reflects many gay men I come across at my events who want to be happy but their behaviour is not allowing them to be. There could be many reasons behind a guy who keeps going for the same, wrong type of man again and again. It could be that the guy in question subconsciously knows that the relationship will not work. Maybe he thinks he does not deserve a functioning, long lasting relationship (see the chapter on self-esteem) or, maybe, he is trapped in the role of the heart broken victim who loves to entertain his friends with his disastrous string of doomed affairs (see the previous chapter on what we attract.) Another theory is that we are subconsciously trying to resolve past issues from our childhood or even searching for men that remind us of our parents. Many relationship therapists suggest we are all looking for partners who have both the positive and negative character traits of our own parents or caretakers in an attempt to feel whole.

A man who lacked a strong father figure or a father who was not present or unloving may seek out a much older partner. A gay man whose childhood lacked discipline may seek a dominant, aggressive mate. Some men who are attracted to much younger guys (who are too young to have a relationship), like Peter, are trying to recapture a lost youth as they came out late and feel they wasted so much time; but he has to realise that a man of 45 does not have the same priorities as a 22 year old. Until he realises this, his relationships will be doomed and the pattern will keep repeating.

Certain men have a very specific physical type which they always go for and put this above everything else. Many therapists argue that we are so deeply impressed by our first love that we continually hold the image of this person as the ideal and try to find a mate that matches him to try to relive the relationship, especially if it ended in tears. For example, some guys only like skinny blond, young guys because their first love looked like that and, no matter who they come across, they always gravitate back to partners with this look. They unconsciously want to go through this first relationship again but this time resolving the issues and having a perfect ending. But, of course, the reasoning mind understands that this is not the same person so nothing gets resolved and a pattern can develop.

Others simply love the drama of stormy relationships- the arguments, tears, breaking and making up. Gay men adore divas who have suffered (especially publicly) like Cher, Britney Spears and Amy Winehouse. Some therapists believe gay men look for passion and conflict in their relationships to make up for the long years they spent alone, repressing their true selves as young adults before they came out. If that is the case for you then maybe you need to listen to a song from another great diva, Mary J Blige, *No more drama in my life*. A relationship should be about mutual respect, support and comfort, not constant fighting and tears. Leave that kind of drama to *Desperate Housewives*; it won't help you in the long run. Amy Winehouse may well use all that publicity to sell records; you don't have to, so break the cycle.

Take some time to examine your previous partners and look for a pattern. Is there a particular type you have been going for again and again? Are there any links you could make with your childhood or upbringing which could explain these choices? Maybe you could consider therapy to understand your behaviour. If therapy seems too extreme then try talking to your closest friends, asking them to be honest with you. Do they see a pattern? We all need to remember that we have control of our lives and our emotions. If you find yourself in some kind of repetitive pattern then you have the power to break it and move on with your life (as all those great divas have done!)

BARRIER No.10: I Can't Get Past the First 2 Months!

Why is it that many gay relationships tend to be so short? This is a question my clients (including Ian, below) have posed many times. So many gay guys complain about not being able to get past the first month or two in their relationships.

Ian, Property Manager, 32.

> *'Well, I', 32 and I am ashamed to say I have never been out with any guy for longer than 6 months. I know it's the same for a lot of my gay friends. Not sure why. I know there's an issue somewhere'.*

We have already looked at the possibility of there being so much choice that many gay guys don't put in the effort for a long term relationship. We also saw how gay men who lack self esteem can sabotage their own relationships because deep down they don't feel worthy enough to be loved or deserve happiness. On top of that, are all the issues many gay guys have not yet resolved from their upbringing. If you put all this in a blender and add a sprinkling of addictions to cruising or sex, then it's not surprising that many gay cannot seem to develop long lasting relationships.

If that doesn't apply to you then what is the reason all your relationships have been so short? As we have seen already, it takes two to tango, so don't blame everything on the other person. Once again, it's time to analyse your past relationships to see if you can spot a pattern but there may also be an unconscious behaviour behind it.

Macho roles

We live in a macho culture where men are socialised to behave a certain way. Men, both gay and straight, are raised to be independent breadwinners who will be able to be strong and provide for a family. We should be sexual predators and hunters. We are raised not to depend on anyone or show any emotion; that is considered a feminine, bad quality. So what happens when you have two men in a relationship together? Sometimes one, or both guys, feel uncomfortable and freak out when they realise they are becoming dependant on another person. According to our social conditioning, this is not supposed to happen. Many guys will try to become less reliant on their partner by working longer hours, staying away from their mate on long work trips or, the gay classic; sleeping around with other men and starting an open relationship. In other words, they destroy the relationship because they cannot deal with their feelings. Not all gay men absorb this macho culture to the same extent. For example, many of my friends have no problem expressing themselves in relationships. My theory is that some families insist on their son going to rugby club, etc and bonding with the boys while others allow their son to follow his own path more. Other boys were sent to all male environments, like boarding schools. Some boys are also influenced by female family members who brought them up and instilled in them a more feminine approach to life and love.

The love drug

Remember that song by Robert Palmer; *Addicted to love* (you remember the video with the pouting girls playing guitars in the background?) You have heard of sex addiction but did you know some people get addicted to the process of falling in love? Scientists have proved that a high-inducing cocktail of hormones including PEA (*phenalethalamine, a natural amphetamine*) is released into our blood when we fall in love.

This natural high can last from a couple of months to a year or so. It can't last any longer as it would place too much stress on the body; imagine all that fast heart beating and eyelash-fluttering going on for twenty years! After this honeymoon period is when the couple get real and the work to keep the relationship going begins. This is nature's way of bringing humans (gay or straight) together. It is easy to see how a gay man who has spent a childhood feeling unloved and alone could become addicted to this rush of love chemicals. But a few months later, when this rush wears off, Mr Love Addict is no longer interested and begins a new search for his next victim. If nobody is getting hurt and Mr Love Addict is happy with a string of short affairs then everything is ok, but as with any other addiction, this may need to be addressed at some stage when he feels the need to move on and experience something longer term.

Conclusion.

We have seen how gay men can often develop issues which hinder them finding suitable partners and developing healthy relationships. While these could range from a slight lack of confidence to huge self-destructive patterns, they all need to be addressed; either with the help of a therapist or relevant reading material. The aim is that the next time you find yourself being attracted to a man who you know is not suitable, or available, or you catch yourself complaining about how unconfident or overweight you are, you stop and say to yourself *'aha! I recognise this pattern!'* and you break the cycle. I promise you that when that moment comes, you will feel ecstatic! From then on, you are free from the past and ready to move forward to an ideal relationship.

It also helps to understand the society and culture that formed our beliefs and attitudes. This enables us to forgive friends or family who have hurt or rejected us in the past; they were just acting out what society has drilled into them. As adults, we can now see the untruths and destructive messages that often surrounded our upbringing for what they really are; nonsense. It's time to work on loving and appreciating yourself more and creating a fulfilling life before Mr Right comes onto the scene. Learning to love your sexuality and what it means, whether you consider yourself as 'straight' acting or effeminate is essential. Sending out a positive self image to others will attract positive people back to you.

It's true that dating is a game and the basic rule is always act like a mature, respectful adult with regards to yourself, your partners and others in your community; treat others as you would like to be treated. We should aim to create a strong, happy place which welcomes gay and lesbian people without the bad attitude and bitchiness that permeates today's gay scene; after all, this behaviour also results from unresolved issues. While gay men in the Western world are lucky to have a strong gay community, they don't have to be confined to it. There is no specific place to meet your future partner, the best approach is to be open and ready to chat to new men anywhere, seeing every opportunity as a chance to make at least a new friend. Whether you are looking for a partner in a bar, on the internet or in the street, remember that body language, positivity and confidence are the keys to success! The internet is a valuable dating tool but it can become addictive and beware of those wasting your time.

At the end of the day, dating comes down to common sense. You know you have to dress well to make an impression and you know not to talk about things that could cause an argument! Enjoy meeting potential partners and relax. Don't stress if you get rejected and remember it's important to make new friends as well as dates. Rejection is part of life and something we all need to accept at some stage or another, it is not the end of the world and nobody should become cold and jaded because of it. Life is too short.

The gay lifestyle offers great freedom, excitement and entertainment. If pressures to conform to, or become obsessed by, certain body images are resisted and sex is not confused with dating, gay men can take advantage of flexible, custom made relationships. We have the amazing luxury of defining our own relationships and living how we choose, creating the rules as we go along. Straight people could learn from that. But, as we have also seen, gay men could also learn a lot from our female friends and family about flirting, dating and not putting the emphasis on sex.

Communication is everything and both parties in a relationship have a responsibility to make themselves clearly heard. Blaming others or acting like a victim is just another barrier which will stop you from finding the right person. So, armed with a new understanding of where you have come from, who you are and what you are looking for, get out there and find your perfect partner! I wish you the very best of luck.

Q& A section

Q: Well, you give some great advice, but, I have to say that all the gay sites I am subscribed to don't have many guys looking for relationships. I do want to settle down but I seriously do not think there are many gay guys out there who think that way. Yes, I have read the section about not being a victim and thinking negatively but you just need to take a look at some of these sites for yourself. It's all about naked photos and dick sizes. How does dating fit into the equation?

A: Firstly, it seems like you are focusing only on internet sites for meeting a partner and 'settling down', as you say. Remember there are other options for meeting gay guys; sports and social groups, through friends etc; so try to examine some other routes. Secondly, although many online profiles are sexual, there are plenty which are not and yours doesn't have to be either. It doesn't matter what other guys are looking for; if your goal is to settle down then that's what your profile should focus on. Maybe you are attracting messages from the wrong type of guys because you are sending the wrong signals out? Make sure your profile states what you are really looking for and doesn't include naked, or even topless, photos. Finally, there are some great gay websites out there where the focus is not sexual; you just need to do a Google search. Happy hunting!

Q: I like many of your ideas in general, but, I have to say that you have painted a picture of gay men's pasts as a bit 'doom and gloom'. I'm 19 years old and I am out to everyone. I didn't have any major problems at school or with my family and I can think of two main soap operas, offhand, that have gay characters. I can also think of a couple of gay politicians. Gay men are not all suffering from complexes and issues.

A: I was delighted to read your mail; I am so happy that you are comfortable with your sexuality and have role models at such a relatively young age. I'm glad you feel this way, but, there are guys your age outside of major cites (or in other countries) where there is less tolerance. This book is also aimed at gay guys of all ages and most guys of 30 or so will have had a different experience of growing up and coming out from the young gay guys of today. You are completely right when you say that not all gay men suffer from complexes and issues; my aim is for readers to take what they need from the book but also to have an understanding of their friends and lovers behaviour.

Q: I am one of those guys you wrote about who gets too excited on dates and probably comes across as a bit desperate. It's easy to say *be like Miranda, cool and calm* in theory; I just can't help it. I can't help obsessing about him when I'm alone and sending him texts. I think it's natural and a good thing to show enthusiasm for somebody you really like, even on a first date.

A: Yes, it's natural to be enthusiastic but you have to contain it or you could scare your date away! Remember that you don't really know each other, even after a couple of great dates. You don't know if he will appreciate being bombarded by texts or not. When you are at home and starting to 'obsess', as you put it (your choice of word seems to imply you are putting unhealthy amounts of attention on him), focus on something else; watch TV, read or concentrate on a hobby. Remember that before looking for a relationship, you need to have a full, balanced, interesting life for yourself. So, if you are only thinking about him in your free time maybe you could build some new interests and hobbies? Take things slowly; there is no need to rush.

Q: Five years ago, I met someone in a sauna and we went out for 3 months. I think sex can lead to something more and I try to use all opportunities as a way of meeting someone for a relationship, whether that be sexual contacts, work or socialising in gay bars. I don't agree with what you say on that point.

A: The good thing is that you see any opportunity as a way to meet a potential partner. Perfect. But, looking for romance in a sauna or with any guy who has just sex on his mind will not get your very far. I see you have only provided one successful example from five years ago. There will always be a one off exception to the rule. What I am trying to get across is that it could be a big waste of time and energy searching for love in the wrong places. Use your common sense and put your efforts into meeting guys who are looking for the same thing as you from the start.

Q: As you pointed out, masculinity is definitely attractive. I have a problem finding gay men who are

really manly though. I've been single for ages. I get so turned off by camp guys or even when I meet a reasonably masculine guy but he says something really gay, I just get so turned off. Where and how can I meet masculine gay guys?

A: First of all, it seems that you need to see the guys you are dating in a holistic way; see their whole personality, body, looks, intelligence and traits together as a whole person rather than being put off by one phrase that you consider too 'gay'. Does that one little phrase or gesture bother you so much that you are willing to dump the rest of, what could be, your perfect package? Don't throw the baby out with the bathwater! It's OK to be turned off by camp guys; different strokes for different folks, as they say. But, it seems like you could also have some issues around masculinity. How do you feel about your own feminine side? Do you try to hide it or did you get teased in the past? You could be searching for a very long time for your Mr Macho because all men have both a masculine and a feminine side; Rambo and the Terminator are not real! You say that you have been single for a long time so this issue seems to be holding you back; don't let it do that to you anymore! Rather than trying to find how and where you can meet masculine guys, try to accept the 'gayness' in yourself and the guys you are dating.

I'm not suggesting that you should be happy to date a drag queen, but see the positive things in the guys you are going out with. Of course, you could just continue your long search, but life is too short. Finally, have you ever considered the impression/ image you are giving out to others? As I mentioned in the book, you should try to dress and act like the person you want to attract.

Q: I'm 36 years old and I realised I was gay around 12 years ago but I have never come out of the closet. You probably think that's really pathetic but I'm scared about my status at work and my family are Orthodox and very religious. I've been out with a string of guys but I dump them when they start pressuring me to come out.

A: Nobody should put pressure on you to do anything you are not comfortable with and nobody should call you pathetic either (yourself included.) Although you are technically living a lie and would surely enjoy healthier relationships if you were out, this is up to you. It is impossible to develop normal, healthy relationships if you are not out of the closet. Living in fear of someone finding out is no atmosphere for dating. There is no rule for coming out and it is a very individual choice; all I can say is that at some stage you *will* have to do it. In my experience, families and friends have normally guessed you are gay already; they put two and two together, especially if you are 36 years old. They may not even be as shocked as you imagine. Despite traditions and religious rules; followers of all faiths love their children unconditionally too!

Try seeing things from your partners perspective too; they probably feel frustrated and, maybe, that you are not serious about the relationship. Think twice before dumping someone on the spur of the moment (you mention you have dumped a string of guys) and try to talk it through with them. If they are out then they can give you valuable support and advice. Even if you decide not to come out, do you want to stay in the closet alone or with somebody who can support you? You could also consider talking to a therapist.

About the Author.

Jaye Sassieni founded Urban Connections, a gay dating website in London, UK, in 2006. Knowledge gained from his degree in Social Science, plus his experience running dating events and dating coaching sessions led to him writing this, his first book, in 2010.

Readers can find out more about Urban Connections at www.urbanconnections.co.uk

The author can be contacted at info@urbanconnections.co.uk

Made in the USA
Monee, IL
02 September 2022